Yorkshire Soccer Heroes

CW00507125

Sheffield United's Ted Burgin saves from Wednesday's Jack Shaw. Burgin later played with Leeds and Doncaster; Shaw is best remembered as a great scoring hero at Rotherham.

Yorkshire Soccer Heroes

by
Keith Farnsworth

Dalesman Books
1988

The Dalesman Publishing Company Ltd.,
Clapham, Lancaster, LA2 8EB
First published 1988
© Keith Farnsworth 1988

ISBN : 0 85206 958 8

Printed by Smiths of Bradford, Bradford, West Yorkshire

CONTENTS

Caricature on page 1 is of Jackie Robinson.

1. Master Managers

Don Revie (Leeds United)

Middlesbrough-born Don Revie first found fame as a deep-lying centre-forward in the mid-1950s. Later he became the game's costliest player when his fourth move, to Leeds in November 1958, brought the total transfer fees paid for him to the then record £83,000. He made over 500 appearances with Leicester, Hull, Manchester City, Sunderland and Leeds, playing in two FA Cup finals and gaining six England caps. However, his achievements as a player were soon eclipsed by his success as a club boss.

In his second term as a player at Leeds they were relegated, and in 1961 he became manager after Jack Taylor's departure. A year later Leeds beat the drop into Division Three by only three points, but by 1963 were promotion contenders and in 1964 were Second Division champions.

In the next ten seasons Leeds won the League Championship (1969 and 1984) and the Fairs Cup (1968 and 1971) twice, and the FA Cup (1972) and the League Cup (1968) once. They also finished First Division runners-up five times (1965, 1966, 1970, 1971, 1972), twice losing in the FA Cup final (1965 and 1970), and once in the Fairs Cup (1967) and the Cup-Winners Cup (1973) finals. In 1970 they were European Cup semi-finalists and in 1975 European Cup finalists.

Under Revie, Leeds were perhaps the most feared team in English football, though not the most popular. On the upward climb they built a reputation as mean and uncompromising, often accused of gamesmanship and intimidation; so though they later emerged as a brilliant, supremely skilful and cultured combination, they never quite erased the old image.

Revie owed much to his dedicated staff, Les Cocker, Sid Owen and Maurice Lindley. Together they bred a club whose success was built on commitment, dedication and unyielding mutual loyalty. The team mattered more than its individual members. Revie, always a clever tactician, also mastered the techniques of management with remarkable rapidity: his attention to detail was a by-word, and he left nothing to chance. Yet he remained excessively superstitious. Someone told him that a gypsy's curse on Elland Road had led to Leeds City's demise and would deny their successors glory; so he engaged another gypsy to lift the curse. Always deeply conscious of omens, perhaps sometimes his preoccupation with Lady Luck tempted ill-fate.

In 1971 when the Championship eluded Leeds by one point, an allegedly off-side goal conceded against West Brom brought unexpected defeat, and provoked a pitch invasion for which Leeds were punished severely. A year later, having won the FA Cup on the Saturday, Leeds lost to Wolves on the Monday and again missed the Championship by a single point and were denied the honour of being the only Yorkshire club to achieve a League and Cup double. Defeat was always a disaster for "The Don", but all the more painful when, as so often was the case, it happened with the elusive prize so close.

Leeds at their peak were often described as "all things white and wonderful" (they played in all-white) and captured their share of records. Between October 1968 and August 1969 they went 34 games without defeat, while in 1973-74 they began the season with an unbeaten run of 29 games, a feat not equalled until Liverpool did it in 1987-88.

Created out of the ashes of the old Leeds City club, United enjoyed modest success in the inter-war years. In three spells in Division One, fifth place in 1930 (under Dick Ray) was their best performance. By 1947 they were back in Division Two. Raich Carter (who had taken Revie to Hull in 1949) led them up again in 1956.

By 1965 Revie had pushed Leeds up to the highest League position in their history and taken them to their first FA Cup final. In 1968 they returned to Wembley to win the League Cup and in 1969 brought the League title to Yorkshire for the first time since Sheffield Wednesday in 1930; while in 1972 they were the first FA Cup winners from Yorkshire for 37 years. But there were setbacks, too: like the Cup KO delivered by Fourth Division Colchester in 1971 and the 1973 Wembley defeat against Second Division Sunderland. Then, of course, there was the heartbreak of the controversial semi-final defeat against Chelsea in 1967. Later, in 1974, came another Cup shock at home to Bristol City, but at least the season ended in triumph with the League Championship captured again.

Revie's success was based on ultra-professional dedication and the creation of a "family" at Leeds. A vital key was the rise of Bremner and the development of such youngsters as Sprake, Harvey, Reaney, Cooper, Madeley, Hunter, Gray and Lorimer, plus such astute signings as Collins (1962), Giles (1963), Jones (1967), Clarke (1969) and Cherry (1972).

In April 1974 Revie left to begin a three-year stint as England's team-chief. Unfortunately, the circumstances in which he deserted the national post for a lucrative job with the United Arab Emirates did not enhance either his reputation or his popularity, and the period was shrouded in controversy and public gossip about his principles and ethics. Elland Road was never quite the same after Revie left.

Brian Clough, another Middlesbrough lad, was his immediate successor, but the man whose Derby County had pipped Leeds for the title in 1972 lasted only 44 days and departed amid allegations that he had been the victim of "player power". Clough went on to build a second Championship side at Nottingham Forest.

In the meantime *Jimmy Armfield* (1974-78) came and went; *Jock Stein* stayed for 44 days in 1978; and *Jimmy Adamson* survived two years before *Allan Clarke* (1980-82) became the first of a trio of Revie old-boys to attempt to revive United's fortunes. But in 1982 Leeds lost their First Division status after 18 years, and despite the efforts of *Eddie Gray* (1982-85) and *Billy Bremner* they have so far failed to climb back. Bremner, who returned via Doncaster Rovers, at least provided a hint of better days in 1987 when he led Leeds to the FA Cup semi-final and the promotion play-offs.

However, in 1988 Leeds were overshadowed in the Second Division promotion race by Yorkshire rivals Middlesbrough and Bradford City (two clubs who literally "came back from the dead"), and a poor start to the 1988/89 campaign led to Bremner's departure in October 1988. His successor was Howard Wilkinson, who moved to Elland Road after five years with Sheffield Wednesday.

John Harris (Sheffield United)

The quiet Scot from Glasgow, John Harris spent 18 years at Bramall Lane, and though as a manager he never captured a League Championship or reached a Wembley final, he is often described as the best of United's chiefs. He twice led United out of Division Two (1961 and 1971); once (1961) took them to an FA Cup semi-final; and steered them to fifth in Division One in 1962. On paper a modest record, perhaps, but his resources were very limited: in truth it was a miracle that he kept United in the top grade so long. He was missed when he left!

In 1975 under *Ken Furphy,* United finished sixth but within a year slumped to relegation,

John Harris, the quiet Scot, was a man of few words but here he finds time to speak to the press. Harris managed Sheffield United and later had a spell with Sheffield Wednesday.

and by 1979 were in Division Three, and by 1981 it was down to Division Four. *Ian Porterfield* led them to the Fourth Division title in 1982 and two years later back into Division Two; but they were soon sliding the wrong way again, and in 1987-88 *Dave Bassett* (the seventh manager since Harris) had the task of trying to save them from another dose of relegation, but down they went.

Harris, the bachelor who always said he was married to football, was born into the game:

the son of Scottish international centre-forward Neil Harris, who played with Partick before scoring 130 goals in 262 League games with Newcastle, Notts County and Oldham and then managing among others Swansea and Swindon. At Swansea in 1934 John Harris began his professional career, first as an inside-forward, then as a centre-half. His father sold him to Spurs in 1939 and he later played with Wolves (where he gained his only cap); but it was at Chelsea that he made his name and gained a League Championship medal in 1955.

Harris never wanted to go into management, but by 1956 he was boss at Chester and in 1959 succeeded Joe Mercer at Bramall Lane. The early 1960s were good years, and, assisted by Archie Clarke, Harris built a reputation for producing many home-grown stars, among them Mick Jones, Bernard Shaw, Birchenall, Badger, Woodward and Salmons. Moreover, he showed an uncanny flair for making bargain signings, as deals involving Len Allchurch, Hartle, Summers, Reece, Currie, Carlin and Dearden illustrated.

Having led United back to Division One and kept them in the top half for some years, Harris was unable to save them from an unexpected fall in 1967-68 (the season he had to sell Jones to Leeds and Birchenall to Chelsea), and he briefly handed over team duties to *Arthur Rowley*. But he was soon back to plot the promotion triumph of 1971. Then in 1973 he again stepped aside, though Furphy's departure in 1975 prompted a suggestion that Harris and coach Cec Coldwell might form a management duo. But it didn't happen. By the time *Jimmy Sirrel* left in September 1977 Harris had joined Wednesday (where he eventually became Jack Charlton's right-hand man and a key figure in the Owl's revival).

After *Harry Haslam* and *Martin Peters* had been and gone, Porterfield, having led Rotherham to the Fourth Division title, arrived to inspire a United climb up two grades; but eventually he fell out of favour. His successor, *Billy McEwan,* suffered a similar fate: so Bassett came, but he couldn't save them from the drop.

Harris, who died at the age of 71 in July 1988 after a long illness, is remembered with affection and gratitude, and is assured of a place in United's hall of fame alongside such earlier long-serving and similarly conservative and publicity-shy chiefs as *John Nicholson* (1899-1932) and *Teddy Davison* (1932-52).

*

Herbert Chapman
(Leeds City and Huddersfield Town)

Looking back now at "master managers" of yesteryear, one who stands out is Herbert Chapman – probably best remembered today as the man who transformed Arsenal into a household name in world football some 60 years ago. Yet he actually made his bow as a League manager with the ill-fated Leeds City before proving himself a master team-builder by piloting Huddersfield Town to glory in the mid-1920s.

Chapman, the miner's son from Kiveton Park, near Rotherham, was never as good a player as his brother, Harry, and after a modest career as an inside-forward whose clubs had included Sheffield United, he was all set to become a mining engineer when he was unexpectedly offered the chance to rejoin Northampton Town as manager. When he led the Cobblers from the foot of the Southern League to the championship within two years it was evident that he had an outstanding flair for soccer management, both in terms of his ability to handle men and his skills as a tactician.

"He was a natural," said Leslie Knighton, a former Huddersfield manager and Chapman's immediate predecessor at Highbury. "There's no doubt about it, the man was a football genius. He had an uncanny instinct for finding promising players, and especially for welding them into good teams. He was exceptionally clever, too, in financial matters, and could talk, as they say, to charm off a donkey's hind leg. No matter what difficulties his directors raised, Herbert could persuade them to his way of thinking."

Roy Goodall, a Huddersfield hero in the 1920s, once told me: "Chapman had a remarkable talent for generating a great team-spirit and for inspiring loyalty. He encouraged a sense of togetherness, not only with revolutionary and imaginative training methods, but with such things as weekly golf outings and team snooker tournaments. He always gave the impression of being very jovial, always had

Herbert Chapman relaxes with his Huddersfield players during FA Cup training in the early 1920s. Snooker was a game he introduced at the club.

a ready smile; but he was shrewd and tough, and you never had any doubt who was boss. He was a hard taskmaster, too, and could be quite ruthless with anyone who went against his code of conduct."

Knighton, the schoolmaster's son from Oughtibridge, near Sheffield, always insisted that Chapman did more for professional football in his time than anyone since William McGregor, the founder of the Football League in 1888. Chapman dreamed of making an essentially working-class game attractive to the cultured classes, and royalty were regular patrons at Highbury after he built a stadium in which spectator comfort mattered. He was the game's first showman, and his ideas, which included floodlit football, the numbering of players, the use of a white ball on murky winter afternoons, and changes in the points and promotion and relegation systems put him years ahead of his time. By the time of his death at the age of 56 in January 1934 he had long been dubbed "the Napoleon of football."

It was in the summer of 1912 (the same time as Arthur Fairclough left FA Cup winners Barnsley for Huddersfield) that Chapman moved back north to succeed F. Scott Walford as manager of Second Division strugglers Leeds City; and after lifting them into the top four within two years he might well have made them a major force in the game had the Great War not intervened. In the event, the war

Harry Chapman, brother of Herbert, had a distinguished playing career with Sheffield Wednesday. He then joined Hull in 1911 and, when injury forced him to hang up his boots, became the club's manager.

proved the making and breaking of Leeds City – and threatened to ruin Chapman's promising career. City twice won the wartime Midland Section championship and in 1918 completed a double by also winning the League Cup. But in 1919 they stood accused of having made illegal payments to guest players, and when they refused to open their books for inspection the Football Association expelled them from the game, with Chapman one of several people banned sine die.

Fortunately, he was able to prove that he had been working at a munitions factory at the time of the alleged irregularities, and his ban was lifted to enable him to attempt to rebuild his career by joining Huddersfield Town as assistant to manager Ambrose Langley, the former Middlesbrough Ironopolis and Wednesday defender.

At the time Town were still recovering from a trauma almost as painful as that experienced by Leeds. In 1919 they had faced financial disaster, and the situation was so bad that there were plans to transfer the club lock, stock and barrel to Leeds. However, a sucessful public appeal saved them at the eleventh hour; and, remarkably, by the end of that 1919-20 season they celebrated by gaining promotion from the Second Division and reaching the FA Cup final. Ironically, the goal which defeated Town in the final came from one of the men sold at the famous Leeds City auction of players seven months earlier!

Town struggled in the First Division and looked likely relegation contenders. But then, in February 1921, Chapman arrived and their fortunes began to improve. Soon afterwards Langley retired to Sheffield and Chapman, in full control, marked his first season as boss by leading Town to victory in the 1922 FA Cup final when they beat Preston 1-0 with a controversial late penalty in the last final played at Stamford Bridge. This triumph was just a beginning, for between 1923 and 1928 Huddersfield were never out of the First Division's top three and clinched a unique hat-trick of League Championships in 1924, 1925 and 1926. The first title in 1924 was claimed in sensational style on the season's last day, Town winning 3-0 while their chief rivals, Cardiff City, missed a penalty and were held to a goalless draw, which meant Chapman's side took the prize by .020 of a goal!

Chapman had the knack of recruiting the right backroom staff – Sheffield chimney sweep Jack Foster became his assistant and chief scout, and Joe Chaplin his trainer – and knew how to play the transfer market. His signing of Clem Stephenson from Aston Villa in 1921 was a stroke of genius. At the time Stephenson was in dispute with Villa because he refused to live in Birmingham, but Chapman was ready to let the England international continue to live in the North East because he knew he was the ideal "old head" and general for his young team. The brilliant inside-forward not only made over 250 appearances but later managed Huddersfield from 1929 to 1942.

Another of Chapman's notable captures at Huddersfield was Scottish international winger, Alex Jackson, signed from Aberdeen in June 1925. However, the "Laughing Cavalier" never actually played for his new manager. A few weeks after completing the deal, Chapman, unable to resist the lure of London and the opportunity it offered, joined Arsenal, and Town actually completed their hat-trick of titles without him.

Huddersfield's managers in the post-war era have included *Andy Beattie, Bill Shankly, Tom Johnston, Ian Greaves* and *Mick Buxton.*

*

Bob Brown (Sheffield Wednesday)

When the Great War ended and "normal" football resumed, Leeds and Huddersfield were not the only Yorkshire crisis clubs. Sheffield Wednesday, oldest of the county's League clubs, endured the worst season in their history in 1919-20 and finished firmly entrenched at the foot of the First Division. The whole business was a nightmare for honorary secretary, Arthur Dickinson, and not surprisingly he decided the time had come for the Owls to recruit a professional secretary-manager. Thus in June 1920 Bob Brown moved in.

Brown had never played League football, but was not unknown to Wednesday. Years before he had been the club's scout in his native North East and had had a spell as Dickinson's assistant in the office. Subsequently he had served a managerial apprenticeship in the Southern League, and his achievements at Portsmouth persuaded Wednesday he was the man for them.

Success, however, did not come easily. It took Brown until 1926 to guide the Owls back

into the First Division; and that was not the end of the gloom, for by early 1928 Wednesday were odds-on favourites for relegation again. But then Brown's luck changed. Picking up 17 points from their last ten games Wednesday miraculously avoided the drop into Division Two. In the next five seasons Wednesday did not once finish below third place in the First Division and within a year of their Great Escape had won the first of two successive League Championships. In 1930 they not only regained the title by a margin of ten points but went close to a League and Cup double, this being the year when they were defeated in the FA Cup semi-final after Huddersfield's Alec Jackson scored a disputed equaliser.

Brown was hailed as a great manager, and it was a major blow when ill-health forced him to quit in the autumn of 1933. His successor was the legendary ex-Aston Villa forward, *Billy Walker,* and when Walker led Wednesday to a memorable FA Cup triumph in 1935 the glory days seemed set to continue. Alas, in 1937 the Owls crashed to relegation, and towards the end of that year Walker left. *Eric Taylor,* another man who had never played League football, eventually led Wednesday back into the top grade in 1950, but the fifties passed into club history as the yo-yo years during which they gained promotion in 1950, 1952, 1956 and 1959, but suffered relegation in 1951, 1955 and 1958.

Harry Catterick steered Wednesday to the Second Division title in 1959, and in 1961 the Owls finished runners-up to Champions Spurs – their highest position since the mid-thirties. Then in 1966 *Alan Brown* piloted Wednesday to the FA Cup final, but after leading Everton 2-0 they slipped to a 2-3 defeat; and by 1970 with *Danny Williams* in charge, they were again on the slide, falling into Division Two. In 1975 they dropped into the Third Division for the first time, and it was not until the arrival of *Jack Charlton* that they began to climb back, returning to the Second Division in 1980. At last, under the leadership of *Howard Wilkinson,* they made it back into the First

A famous Rotherham trio. Manager Reg Freeman (centre) with Mark Hooper (left) and Andy Smailes. Hooper and Smailes both played for Sheffield Wednesday; Smailes later managed Rotherham.

Division in 1984. Since then the Owls have finished as high as fifth and never below thirteenth, but the departure of Howard Wilkinson in late 1988 was a disappointment and his move to Leeds served to show that Wednesday have to fight to maintain their place as Yorkshire's premier club!

Managerial Round-up

After *Arthur Fairclough* led Barnsley to their great 1912 FA Cup triumph he joined Huddersfield. Later, after a spell at Leeds, he returned to Oakwell, where his successors have included *Angus Seed* (1937-53) and *Johnny Steele*, who came as a player in 1938, stayed to serve as coach, manager from 1960 to 1971, and later general manager and secretary.

Dick Ray managed Doncaster Rovers and Leeds before succeeding *Jack Peart* at Bradford City, while *David Menzies* started at Bradford City and finished at Doncaster after a stay in Hull. *Bob Brocklebank,* too, served both Bradford City and Hull; and *Willie Watson* had one spell at Valley Parade and two at Halifax, where his most successful successors have probably been *Alan Ball Snr* and *George Kirby.*

Cliff Britton (his predecessors included Bill McCracken and Percy Lewis) spent ten good years at Hull, where their most famous player-manager was *Raich Carter,* who guided them into Division Two in 1949. Carter took Leeds into Division One in 1956 (he followed Maj. Frank Buckley at Hull and Leeds) and then managed Middlesbrough.

Tom Johnston had two spells at Huddersfield and also managed Rotherham and York, taking Rotherham to their first-ever League Cup final (1961) and Huddersfield to the League Cup semi-final (1968); but perhaps his greatest triumph was in guiding York into the Second Division in 1974. Bootham predecessors included the long-serving *Tom Mitchell* and *Tom Lockie;* a notable successor was *Dennis Smith* with *John Bird* the present chief.

Several Revie old-boys have managed two Yorkshire clubs. *Jack Charlton* led Middlesbrough into Division One in 1974 and Wednesday into Division Two in 1980. *Allan Clarke* shot Barnsley into Division Three in 1979, then had a spell at Leeds before returning to Oakwell. In the meantime, old pal *Norman Hunter* pushed Barnsley into Division Two in 1981 before moving to Rotherham.

Middlesbrough's many notable managers include *Peter McWilliam,* who in 1927 arrived as the game's highest-paid manager at £1,500 a year and twice led 'Boro to the Second Division title. Forty years on and *Stan Anderson* was as much a hero when he steered them out of Division Three: though the achievement of Bruce Rioch in guiding 'Boro from Division Three and the shadow of bankruptcy to triumph in the 1988 play-offs and a return to Division One was truly tremendous.

It was at Middlesbrough that *Reg Freeman* made his name as a full-back, but his chief claim to fame was as Rotherham United's manager. At Millmoor from 1930, and player-manager from 1934, in 1951 he finally led United to the Third Division (North) title before joining Sheffield United. Freeman's successor, *Andy Smailes,* a Millmoor "fixture" from 1932 to 1958 as player, trainer and then manager, almost led them into Division One in 1955, but a missed penalty in their final game cost them promotion on goal-average.

Freeman discovery *Danny Williams* managed Rotherham from 1962 to 1965 and was later with Sheffield Wednesday. *Jim McGuigan* it was who led Rotherham out of Division Four in 1975, while *Ian Porterfield* piloted them to the Third Division title in 1981 before joining Sheffield United. Porterfield's successor at Bramall Lane, *Billy McEwan,* moved to Rotherham in 1988.

Doncaster's many managers include *David Menzies, Jackie Bestall* and *Peter Doherty,* who all led them to the Third Division (North) title; plus *Bill Leivers, Lawrie McMenemy* and *Billy Bremner,* who steered them out of Division Four.

At Bradford City in 1911 *Peter O'Rourke's* team were the first winners of the present FA Cup and finished fifth in Division One; but modern followers probably honour more such recent managers as *Jimmy Wheeler, Bobby Kennedy, Trevor Cherry, Roy McFarland* and especially *Terry Dolan.* After traumatic off-the-field dramas, City's rise from the Fourth to within touching distance of the First in the 1980s was a source of wonder and delight, and Dolan's 1987-88 performance assures him of a place alongside Valley Parade's managerial giants of yesteryear. What a shame they should be pipped for promotion in the play-offs, and how ironic that their dream of a return to the top grade after 66 years should be shattered by another Yorkshire club.

2. Star Captains

Ernest Needham (Sheffield United)

Sheffield United, founded in 1889 and elected to the Football League three years later, were one of the sensations of English soccer in the last decade of the Victorian era, enjoying a sustained spell of success which they have never since equalled. After winning promotion from the Second Division at the first attempt in 1893, they were First Division runners-up in 1897 (and again in 1900) and League Champions in 1898; and then played in three FA Cup finals in four years, winning the trophy twice, in 1899 and 1902.

At one stage they had a dozen internationals on their books, including that trio of huge defenders Foulke, Thickett and Boyle; but the giant of the team in terms of pure genius was one of its smallest members – 5ft 5¾in. *Ernest Needham,* the Staveley product hailed by his contemporaries as "the prince of half-backs" and almost certainly the most successful captain United ever had.

Slight in build, Needham was nevertheless a tower of strength and a source of constant inspiration; a "natural" with outstanding ball skills and tremendous stamina and a "born" leader. He said he owed much to the early influence of veteran Scot Bill Hendry, club skipper when he arrived at Bramall Lane at the age of 18 in 1891; but, in truth, encouragement and experience were all the youngster needed.

Needham had shone as a boy among men in Staveley's Midland League side before joining United, and from his earliest days displayed a knack of dispossessing bigger and heavier opponents with a seemingly gentle shoulder charge. That skill quickly earned him the nickname "Nudger", and he remained ever fearless, a great competitor never happier than when in the thick of the action at both ends of the field.

The quality which made him exceptional from the outset was his talent for leadership. He thrived on responsibility. Thus he was at his best on those occasions when the odds

Ernest Needham – a great captain.

against his side were at their highest. "Leave it to me!" was his constant battle cry as he took charge of a situation and rallied his "troops". In those days before the modern concept of managers and coaches, the skipper was usually responsible for tactics and for adapting to situations as they arose during a match. Needham's strength was not so much his tactical flair as his sheer determination. He simply refused to admit defeat, and when he was playing no game was lost until the final whistle.

Needham collected 16 England caps and played ten times for the English League; and perhaps his proudest moment came in 1901 when he captained England against Wales – a rare honour in those days when amateurs were usually preferred. When his first-team days ended in 1910 he played briefly with the reserves and in one game against Leeds City was given a tough time by a young Irish lad who showed no respect for Needham's reputation. "Nudger" didn't enjoy the experience but recognised a player of exceptional promise and urged Secretary John Nicholson to sign him. The youngster eventually became another famous United captain. His name was Billy Gillespie.

Footnote: Needham was the first of a number of players from Yorkshire clubs to captain England. Others included George Wilson, Ernest Blenkinsop and Alf Strange (Wednesday), Roy Goodall and Sam Wadsworth (Huddersfield), and Willis Edwards (Leeds). It is probably worthy of note that one of the greatest of club captains, *Clem Stephenson*, the hero of Huddersfield in the 1920s, collected only one England cap.

*

Billy Gillespie (Leeds City and Sheffield United)
Before the Great War, Leeds City manager Frank Scott-Walford unearthed a rich seam of soccer talent in Ireland, and among the many youngsters he took to Elland Road was a teenage centre-forward called Billy Gillespie, a lad destined to become one of the game's most

---

George Utley
Barnsley and Sheffield United

It was in 1908 that George Utley arrived at Barnsley and quickly became a battling but perceptive half-back. Five years later he joined Sheffield United for a fee of £2,000 – then the highest in football history. In 1922 he went to Manchester City and later completed a unique sporting career as a cricket instructor at Rossall School.

---

famous captains. However, it was at Sheffield and not Leeds that he climbed to fame.

The son of a Londonderry policeman, Gillespie became a professional footballer against his father's wishes, and at first it seemed his career might not be blessed with success, for despite ten goals in 24 senior outings for Leeds he was largely confined to the second team. Fortunately, in one reserve game he faced former England man Ernest Needham and proved such a handful that old "Nudger" recommended him to Sheffield United secretary John Nicholson; and in December 1911 Gillespie moved to Bramall Lane, where he was to remain for 20 years, making almost 500 League and Cup appearances and scoring 139 goals.

Yet, as he revealed years later, his United career nearly didn't begin. "The deal might easily have been called off before it was signed and sealed," he chuckled. "Scott-Walford had told me to ask for £4 a week, which was then the maximum wage, but old Nicholson wouldn't budge from £3. I stuck it out, but when Nicholson suddenly left the office I thought I'd lost my chance. Fortunately, when he returned he said the directors had agreed to pay £4 – but only when I was in the first-team."

Gillespie made sure he got in the team and stayed there. In his first 17 games he bagged 14 goals, scoring one on his debut and following up with a three and a four; and by 1913 his form had earned him the first of his 25 Irish caps, which he celebrated by scoring both goals in Ireland's first-ever defeat of England. But just when life was looking good, misfortune struck. In September 1914 Gillespie broke a leg and thus missed United's 1915 FA Cup triumph.

The injury threatened his future and only skilled surgery and the insertion of a metal plate in the leg saved his career.

With the departure of George Utley in 1922, Gillespie took over as United's captain, and a year later became Ireland's skipper. By now he had switched to inside-forward, and though still a frequent marksman he emerged as one of the game's cleverest schemers, a leader with the knack of blending a team into a very effective unit.

In 1923 and 1928 United reached the FA Cup semi-final and in 1924 and 1926 finished fifth in Division One. In between, in 1924-25, Gillespie and United had an unforgettable sea-

Sheffield United captain Billy Gillespie shows off the FA Cup after the team's return from Wembley in 1925.

son when he played in his 18th international to become Sheffield's most-capped player and then led United to a memorable FA Cup triumph at Wembley. In that final he showed his true genius as a tactician.

The great feature of United's team at this time was the left-wing triangle of Green, Gillespie and Tunstall, and Tunstall's lethal shooting made him among the most feared wingers in the game. Gillespie, knowing that opponents Cardiff City would pay extra attention to United's left flank, deliberately "starved" Tunstall for a long spell and forced attacks from the right led by Pantling, Mercer and Boyle. Then, suddenly, he switched play to the left, fed Tunstall a dream of a pass, and the little winger burst through to score the game's only goal.

Gillespie enjoyed many glorious moments in Belfast and Sheffield, but he had his off-days, too, especially later in his career, and there were times when he escaped the wrath of waiting supporters by slipping out of the ground at the cricket pavilion end! Yet he will always be remembered as one of Bramall Lane's true giants, his balding head and long shorts symbols of the kind of skill and influence which were often absent after he bowed from the scene. United's fortunes fell into decline in the post-Gillespie years, and while they have had some outstanding captains in the past 50 years – among them George Green, Jimmy Hagan and Joe Shaw – none succeeded in leading the Blades to another Cup triumph, though Harry Hooper led them to Wembley in 1936 when they were unlucky to lose to Arsenal. Tom Johnson led United back into the top grade in 1939 after they had fallen into Division Two for the first time in 41 years following Gillespie's departure.

*

Jimmy Seed (Sheffield Wednesday)

Wednesday have had many excellent captains: Jack Earp in the 1890s, Ambrose Langley and Tommy Crawshaw soon afterwards, Ronnie Starling of the 1935 FA Cup-winning side and

Tommy Crawshaw – an excellent captain of Sheffield Wednesday.

Don Megson of the 1966 team, just to mention a few. But one skipper has passed into club folklore: Jimmy Seed, who led them from gloom to the glorious Championship triumphs of 1929 and 1930.

It will never be forgotten that Seed inspired the club's Great Escape from relegation just before they were transformed into champions. In 1928 Wednesday looked doomed when they stood seven points adrift of their nearest rivals at the foot of Division One with ten matches left; but then they turned the form book upside down and collected 17 of a possible 20 points to beat the drop by the skin of their teeth.

Seed was considered so vital to the side that he often played when he wasn't fit. His mere presence was considered enough. "If you can't play, Jimmy," said manager Bob Brown, "just throw your shirt on to the pitch!"

John Harris, the old Sheffield United chief, often called football a "funny game", and certainly it is full of unexpected coincidences and strange twists of fate. Seed's story is a classic example. For instance, if Spurs manager Peter McWilliam had not been lured to Middlesbrough to become the game's highest-paid manager in February 1927, Seed might not have left White Hart Lane. When McWilliams's successor, Billy Minter, cut his wages by £1 a week, Seed wanted to hang up his boots immediately and become a manager; and, after being pipped for the Leeds job by Dick Ray, he was set to join Aldershot – only to be refused his release by Spurs.

Minter preferred to use him as a makeweight in the deal which took Wednesday's Darkie Lowdell to London. Seed moved to Sheffield, but didn't expect to succeed – though as Spurs clearly considered him "over the hill" he had every reason to want to prove them wrong.

In later years Seed always insisted that he never really excelled at Hillsborough, and was surprised at the fame and adulation his four-year stay brought him. At the time Wednesday, having returned to the First Division in 1926, were struggling, and Brown, searching for an "old head" to guide his young team, was delighted when Seed became available. But Seed did not begin well and just when he was finding his feet he suffered a fractured rib. Meanwhile, Wednesday slipped further and further down the table, until by mid-March the situation looked hopeless.

However, a few weeks earlier, developments occurred which eventually prompted a revival. When skipper Kean lost his place to young Leach the captaincy passed to Seed, and gradually results improved. In late March they began a ten-match run which brought seven victories (including an Easter double over Spurs) and a dramatic last-day win lifted Wednesday to safety leaving the relegated pair

none other than McWilliam's Middlesbrough and Seed's old club Spurs!

In the midst of all the gloom of early 1928, Bob Brown somehow created the blend which turned Wednesday into championship material. Within 12 months they had landed their first League title for 25 years, and in 1930 they not only regained the title by a margin of ten points but reached the FA Cup semi-finals. Seed, now 35, went on to complete nearly 150 games and bring his Owls goal-tally to 37 before finally fulfilling his wish to be a manager.

Seed was a man who had come back twice, for after being gassed in the Great War he was released by Sunderland before reviving his career at Mid-Rhondda. At Tottenham he collected five England caps and became one of the most respected players in the game. Only Seed would have dared to send a referee off the field (as he did during a Glasgow-Sheffield game) because the official's shirt clashed with his team's colours!

After leaving Sheffield, Seed enjoyed a memorable 23-year spell as manager of Charlton Athletic, and his brother became a manager, too. When Spurs refused to let Jimmy become Aldershot's team-boss in 1927, he recommended Angus for the job. Had that not happened, perhaps Angus would not have later enjoyed a 16-year stint as manager of Barnsley.

*

Willis Edwards, Bobby Collins and Billy Bremner (Leeds United)

The success Leeds enjoyed under Don Revie eclipsed all their previous achievements, but when Collins and Bremner were being hailed as United's greatest captains older supporters recalled the talents of Willis Edwards.

In his time, they said, Edwards was as good a player and skipper as anyone in the game: the first United man to play for England, and captain in the last of his 16 internationals between March 1926 and November 1929.

True, at club level the major honours eluded him, but that fate has befallen many giants. Probably the best right-half of his time, Edwards was a brilliantly creative all-rounder: good with his head, superb when it came to trapping and controlling the ball, and one of the best passers around. In short, he was a delight to watch, and a fine skipper, too.

He was the second Derbyshire product to captain United, the first being Jim Baker, the Ilkeston lad who arrived via Huddersfield in 1920 and made 200 appearances during which he led Leeds to the Second Division title in 1924. A year before Baker left in 1926, Edwards had been signed for £1,500 from Chesterfield and had already collected two caps.

Edwards had his share of setbacks, for Leeds were relegated in 1927 and again in 1931 (only a year after finishing fifth), but only 60 of his 400-plus League appearances up to 1939 were in the Second Division. His brief spell as manager at Elland Road coincided with United's early post-war decline, but he remained a member of the training staff until 1960; and thus was present when both Revie and schoolboy Bremner arrived to signal the start of a new era.

The capture of Bobby Collins in late 1962 was a masterstroke, for the 5ft 4in. "pocket-sized general", then 31, went on to make a major contribution to United's initial rise under Revie. Collins had spent ten years at Celtic and nearly five at Everton, but there was still plenty of football left in him, and he made almost 170 appearances in the next five years.

As in the cases of Stephenson at Huddersfield and Seed at Sheffield Wednesday, Collins was the wise older head who inspired and guided his younger colleagues. Leeds took the Second Division title in 1964, and when a year later they finished Division One runners-up and defeated FA Cup finalists few were surprised when Bobby's form earned him an international recall as well as the Footballer of the Year trophy.

After Collins left, his successor as skipper was another pint-sized Scot, the 5ft.5in. red-

Willis Edwards (*Leeds United*).

haired Billy Bremner, who had started as a forward but developed into a brilliant right-sided midfielder (or what Willis Edwards would have called a right-half!). Bremner was one of the game's cleverest and most competitive players, but his weakness was his fiery temper; and many remember his confrontations with the likes of Dave Mackay (immortalised in a famous photograph) and his sending off (with Keegan) in a Charity Shield game. But making Bremner captain was another inspired decision, for he matured with responsibility, and if he never lost that explosive temperament his terrific drive and determination were the epitome of the Leeds brand of professionalism, and the little Scot was a tremendous inspiration to his team-mates.

Bremner was to chalk up 768 League and Cup appearances and score over 100 goals, and with 54 games for Scotland (many as captain) he became United's most-capped player. Having played in the promotion side of 1964 and the 1965 Cup final team, Bremner led Leeds to the League title in 1969 and 1974, the FA Cup triumph of 1972 and the League Cup success of 1968; and he played, too, in some 70 Cup games in Europe. But abroad as well as at home he tasted the extremes of fortune. The "double" eluded Leeds more than once when it was within touching distance, as in 1970 when Bremner's consolation was the Footballer of the Year trophy.

Bremner left Leeds in 1976 and after a spell at Hull began his managerial apprenticeship at Doncaster before returning to United in 1985. Alas, he was unable to pilot Leeds back to Division One and in late 1988 he was axed.

A Sheffield United side of 1902 – note the giant goalkeeper Willie Foulke in the middle of the back row. Sitting at "inside-right" is Alf Common, later sold by Middlesbrough for £1,000 in 1905.

3.   The Boys "Between the Sticks"

"Fatty" Foulke
(Sheffield United)

In their 100 years' existence Sheffield United have had some excellent and colourful goalkeepers. However, when it comes to "characters", the greatest of them all must surely be William "Fatty" Foulke (1894-1905), the 6ft 1in. and 20-stone-plus Shropshire-born and Derbyshire-raised giant who played in some 340 games, gained one England cap, and helped United win the League Championship and two out of three FA Cup finals. "Little Willie" appeared in 41 cup matches and finished on the losing side only seven times.

Foulke, who had arms resembling huge legs of lamb, could clutch the hardest shots with one hand, making it look as easy as catching a cricket ball; and it was quite normal for him to punch the ball beyond the halfway line with his fist. Little wonder that opposing forwards didn't venture close at corner-kicks. And, of course, when it came to spot-kicks Foulke's huge frame didn't offer a penalty-taker much space to aim at!

Yet many a brave opponent attempted to fell the mighty goalkeeper, knowing perhaps that, tough as he was, Foulke didn't like to be niggled. One Aston Villa forward tried to shoulder charge Willie once too often, failed to connect, and finished upside down in the goal with his feet caught in the netting. Foulke scoffed at his pleas for help: "Tha got thissen up there, tha mun get thissen down!"

On another occasion, Liverpool giant George Allan made a point of clattering into Foulke at every opportunity. In the end the exasperated goalkeeper picked Allan up and, to the astonishment of the crowd, stood him on his head in the muddy goalmouth! Foulke was most aggrieved when the referee awarded Liverpool a penalty; and, as in another instance when he was similarly punished for throwing a Port Vale man into the back of the net, "Little Willie" first remonstrated with the official and then refused to make any attempt to save the penalty-kick!

For such a huge man Foulke was remarkably agile, though once when his agility enabled him to make a terrific diving save he pulled a muscle and was unable to get up off the ground. It took no fewer than six men to raise him and carry him off for attention. Whenever he fell to the ground in attempting a save the ground invariably seemed to shudder, and on those occasions when the pitch was a quagmire after rain Foulke was said to resemble a great whale, with water spouting from beneath him in all directions!

An old United director, Tom Bott, once said that Foulke seldom ate more than a slice of toast on the morning of a match, preferring a tot of brandy to calm his nerves. However, at other times his appetite was insatiable. Once, for instance, during special training at the seaside, he stayed behind while his team-mates went for an early-morning stroll. When they returned they found him slumbering in a corner of the hotel dining room having eaten every one of the fifteen breakfasts set out by the waiter!

One of the most famous Foulke tales concerned the 1902 FA Cup final, in which Southampton grabbed a controversial equaliser three minutes before the final whistle. In

Charles Sutcliffe, a Yorkshire favourite of the 1920s.

the dressing room afterwards Foulke was still complaining "the goal was miles off-side" and suddenly dashed off in search of referee Tom Kirkham. The sight of the 20-stone giant storming down the corridor in his birthday suit alarmed the stewards, and Mr. Kirkham, forewarned of the approach of his naked visitor, had the sense to lock himself in his cubicle!

Foulke shared in some of the greatest mo-

ments in United's early history, but there were times when his super confidence and considerable weight made him rather vulnerable to a counter-attack. When United were sensationally defeated in a Cup-tie at Port Vale in 1898, Vale's winning goal came when Foulke was caught standing on the halfway line and lost the chase back to his goal. The sight of the puffing Willie pursuing a speedy little opponent must have been very amusing for everyone except the United team!

The Foulke era came to a sudden end when he conceded ten goals in two games, and after Lievesley took over he moved on, first to Chelsea and then Bradford City. Later he became a publican but fell upon hard times, and while running a shooting gallery on Blackpool sands ("Try to beat the famous Foulke") he caught a fatal chill. When he died in 1916 he was only 41.

Later United heroes included *Jack Smith, Ted Burgin* and *Alan Hodgkinson* (652 games), with *Harold Gough* (1913-24) perhaps the greatest "character" after Foulke.

*

Reginald Garnet (Tim) Williamson (Middlesbrough)

After Middlesbrough joined the Football League in 1899, it took them just three years to climb out of the Second Division. They spent the next 18 seasons in Division One, and throughout that period (which because of the Great War actually spanned 22 years) their goalkeeper was that remarkable Yorkshireman, R. G. Williamson, always known as Tim and hailed as one of the game's all-time greats.

Williamson, born at North Ormsby in 1884, made 563 League appearances for 'Boro and for a long spell was not only a master goalkeeper but an excellent skipper. Ever the great enthusiast, in his early days he often played for his local team, Redcar Crusaders, in the morning and Middlesbrough in the afternoon. A thoughtful, studious and dedicated professional, he was so skilled in all branches of the art of goalkeeping that he made the job look deceptively easy; and his imperturbability and composure under pressure inspired confidence in his colleagues.

In his first years he was the youngest goalkeeper in the League but already one of the best; and it was no surprise when he became Middlesbrough's first home-produced English international in 1905. However, it was a source of much dismay that he has to wait until 1911 for his second cap. In seven games for England he was on the losing side only once – against Ireland in his last international in 1913.

When Williamson retired in 1923 to concentrate on his other career as a draughtsman his departure saw 'Boro endure mixed fortunes, starting with the painful fall of 1924. His eventual successor, *Jimmy Mathieson,* from Raith, helped 'Boro win the Second Division title twice (1927 and 1929) during a run of 250 games; while a later import from Aberdeen, *David Cumming,* played only in the top grade and was good enough to win a Scottish cap against England in 1938.

Since 1946 Middlesbrough's goalkeepers have included former Wednesday man *Derek Goodfellow* and Italian-born naturalised Scot *Rolando Ugolini,* who arrived in 1948 from Glasgow Celtic and went on to make 320 League appearances before leaving for Wrexham in 1957. By then 'Boro had fallen from the First Division. *Peter Taylor,* who played in some 140 games and subsequently earned fame as Brian Clough's partner in management at Derby, was Ugolini's successor.

Willie Whigham arrived from Falkirk in 1966 in time to help 'Boro climb out of Division Three under Stan Anderson's management, and he went on to play in some 200 games before being succeeded by *Jim Platt.* Missing only two matches in the Second Division championship triumph of 1974, Ballymena-born Platt eventually chalked up 400 League appearances and brought his tally of Irish caps to 23.

But 'Boro suffered another fall in 1980s, and ex-Manchester United apprentice *Stephen Pears* was the team's last line of defence in the

Sheffield United's long-serving goalkeeper, Alan Hodgkinson (1954-71).

dramatic bid for another return to Division One in 1988.

*

Some Hillsborough Heroes

Funny game, football. One day you're King of the Kop, the next a fallen idol and goalkeepers know better than most how fickle fortune can be. *Martin Hodge* certainly knows. In early 1987 he claimed the record for consecutive appearances which pre-war winger Mark Hooper had held for 55 years; but by early 1988 he had been dropped, and supporters showed him little sympathy. A man is only as good as his last performance!

Hodge joined Wednesday in 1983. He arrived at the same time as Iain Hesford, and those who knew that Hesford's father, Bob, had been a famous Huddersfield goalkeeper thought he rather than Hodge would emerge first choice. In the event, Hesford didn't play one senior game, while Hodge began a run of 214 matches; and in that spell performed splendidly to help Wednesday win promotion from the Second Division and consolidate their position in the top grade.

The club captaincy soon passed to Hodge, and his success saw him placed on stand-by for England's 1986 World Cup squad. Then came a sudden loss of confidence. A couple of "soft" goals put Hodge under fire, Wednesday's run of poor results didn't help his cause, and after some 250 games as an automatic choice he was displaced by young Kevin Pressman.

After the likes of *Teddy Davison* and *Jack Brown* pre-war, Wednesday couldn't boast a goalkeeper of International Class until *Ron Springett* arrived in 1958. Londoner Springett made 384 appearances and with 33 games for England became the club's most-capped player, being perhaps the best of all Owls' goalkeepers. However, the club honours eluded him except for the 1959 Second Division championship and a place in the 1966 FA Cup final side. In 1967 he returned to QPR in the unique exchange deal which took younger brother, Peter, to Hillsborough.

Peter had helped QPR win the League Cup in 1967 but found the prizes more elusive at Hillsborough. With 207 outings he lifted the Springett brothers' joint tally of games for Wednesday to nearly 600, but while Ron played in a team which was generally successful Peter joined a side on the slide. After the

fall into Division Two, for some years he faced the rivalry of two other Peters, Grummitt and Fox, and when he left in 1975 Wednesday were booked for Division Three. Peter went on to play some 200 games for Barnsley.

Chris Turner later became the first Sheffield-born goalkeeper to claim a regular place in the Owls' League side, but it was Dover-born *Bob Bolder* who was "between the sticks" in the Division Three promotion run of 1980.

. . . and some other South Yorkshire Stars

Goalkeepers are a breed apart, often regarded as slightly crazy for taking on the job. This was especially so in those days when they had precious little protection and opposing forwards delighted in bundling both the goalkeeper and the ball into the back of the net. Yet, on the whole, they have always been great survivors, and any list of long-serving players invariably includes plenty of goalkeepers.

At Barnsley, *Tommy Gale* (who came from Harrogate in 1922) chalked up some 300 appearances in nine seasons; while Chapeltown-product *Harry Hough* registered over 350 between 1947 and 1958 before concluding his career at Bradford Park Avenue. *Ken Hardwick* (1946-56) played in well over 300 matches for Doncaster Rovers, while *John Quairney* (1948-59) topped 260 outings with Rotherham.

Gale is remembered as one of the best of Oakwell's line of goalkeepers, but many insist that the greatest of all was *Jack Cooper,* who arrived from Sutton in 1908, went on to play in some 200 games, and helped Barnsley to win the FA Cup in 1912. *Tom Ellis,* who came from Middlesbrough in the 1930s, and *Clifford Binns,* a member of the 1939 promotion side, are others often recalled with affection. However, perhaps Barnsley's outstanding goalkeeping "character" was *Tom Thorpe.*

Thorpe arrived in 1905, missed out on the FA Cup runs of 1910 and 1912 because he left to join Herbert Chapman's Northampton, but returned to Oakwell briefly in 1921 before retiring to concentrate on his business at

Ron Springett – a fine goalkeeper in action.

Kilnhurst. One of the first goalkeepers to make a mark as a penalty-taker, he is often remembered for his wit and humour. When Barnsley played in a Cup-tie at Everton in 1909, he visited the home dressing room and asked to see the boots of free-scoring Bert Freeman. Thorpe chalked on the soles of the boots "no goals today". Sure enough, Freeman failed to score, but, unfortunately, Thorpe still conceded three goals!

Hough was certainly one of Barnsley's best-ever goalkeepers, and he was decidedly unfortunate not to gain many representative honours. His immediate predecessor, *Pat Kelly*

(150 appearances, 1946-50), at least had the pleasure of being capped by Ireland – not bad for a man who was born in South Africa and arrived at Oakwell from Scotland!

Some goalkeepers are more prone to injuries than others. *Alan Hill* (1960-65) was unlucky in this way, and the jinx followed him first to Rotherham and then Nottingham Forest. Hill's successor at Oakwell was *Roy Ironside*, who, ironically, had played in some 220 League matches for Rotherham (1956-64) before moving to Barnsley. At Rotherham, Ironside had followed in a Millmoor line which included Warnes. Quairney and Bolton. *George*

Warnes, a Thurcroft product, enjoyed a great run between 1944 and 1948, but it was another local lad, *Ron Bolton,* who was in goal when the Millers finally clinched the Third Division (North) title in 1951. Later Bolton lost his place to Scot Quairney.

There has always been great rivalry between goalkeepers at a club, and one example among countless others is provided by the case of *"Ike" Tate* and *Jim Imrie* at Doncaster in the 'thirties. Tate looked set for a long run when he arrived from West Ham in 1929, but during the Division Three (North) championship campaign of 1934-35 he lost his place to Imrie, who had come from Kettering in 1933. By the time of Rovers' next title triumph in 1947 the green jersey had passed to ex-Raith Rovers man *Archie Ferguson;* but soon afterwards West Auckland product *Ken Hardwick* regained his place and kept it for several years during one of the most exciting periods in Doncaster's history.

The best remembered of the Belle Vue discoveries after the war was Hardwick's successor, *Harry Gregg.* After about 100 games for Rovers between 1952 and 1957, Gregg hit the headlines with his £25,000 transfer to Manchester United. He survived the Munich air crash and went on to collect 24 Irish caps as well as playing in the 1958 FA Cup final.

*

East and West Riding Favourites
The Milburns were not the only relatives of Jack Charlton's to precede him at Leeds. There was also *Jimmy Potts,* who married a Milburn sister. Potts, a native of Ashington, joined Leeds from Blyth in 1925 and gave splendid service with some 260 appearances before moving on to Port Vale in 1934. A later rival to Potts in terms of popularity was *Royden Wood,* who arrived in 1952 from Clitheroe and played in more than 200 games before retiring in 1959 and becoming a betting shop manager.

All earlier heroes were overshadowed by the achievements of *Gary Sprake* (1961-73) and *David Harvey* (1965-85), who between them played in some 950 League and Cup matches for United. Sprake made his debut at 16 and gained the first of his 37 Welsh caps at the age of 18; and, apart from the odd clanger, proved himself an outstanding goalkeeper. After some 500 appearances he joined Birmingham for £100,000, and Harvey, who had waited patiently in the shadows, emerged as a ready-made star. Indeed, such was his impact that he soon collected the first of his 16 Scottish caps.

More recently United have had the services of *John Lukic,* who went on to play for Arsenal; and *Mervyn Day,* who began his career in London with West Ham but later found Elland Road much to his liking.

Huddersfield's long tradition for notable goalkeepers dates back to *Sandy Mutch,* who played in the FA Cup finals of 1920 and 1922; but their first genuine giant in the position was *Ted Taylor,* one of the finest signings ever made by Herbert Chapman. Taylor collected League Championship medals in 1924 and 1926, and six England caps; and when he was unexpectedly sidelined during the 1924-25 campaign Chapman recruited a very capable deputy from Hull City, *Billy Mercer.*

After Taylor's departure, *Hugh Turner* became a "fixture" for eleven years, playing in the 1930 FA Cup final and gaining two England caps. Turner's patient understudy was schoolteacher *Bob Hesford,* who soon proved himself master of the art of goalkeeping. Hesford took over in 1937, within a year was playing in an FA Cup final, and but for the war might well have registered more than his 300 appearances.

Town's post-war goalkeepers have included *Johnny Wheeler,* a member of that fine team of the early 1950s; *Ray Wood* (1958-64), the former Manchester United man who played in over 200 games; and *John Oldfield, Terry Poole* and *David Lawson.*

When one thinks of Hull City goalkeepers the first name that comes to mind is *Billy Bly,* a "fixture" at the club in more than 400 games until his career finally ended in the late 1950s. More recently came *Ian McKechnie,* with some 250 outings between 1966 and 1973; and *Jeff Wealands* (1970-78) with 240 League appearances.

Mention of Bradford always brings to mind the tragic decline of the Park Avenue club, and one remembers *Tom Farr,* the goalkeeper whose career began in the late 1930s and continued until 1950, playing in over 500 games. Farr was the first goalkeeper I ever saw rush out of his penalty area to head the ball! Younger supporters still recall *John Hardie* (1963-69), who played in some 270 games; and they are sure to remember that *Mitchell Downie* totted up more than 150 appearances with Park Avenue in the early 1950s and later went in to play in nearly as many with Bradford City. *Pat Liney* also had a few games with Park Avenue before registering some 150 with the other Bradford club.

Geoff Smith played in over 250 games with Bradford City in the 1950s, while *Alex Smith* managed around 100 for City in the 1960s before going on to make 341 League appearances for Halifax between 1967 and 1975. Mention of Halifax reminds us that *Arthur Johnson* clocked up 200-plus games for them in the mid-1950s, while later *Peter Downsborough* managed about 100 before enjoying notable success at Swindon.

York, too, have had some fine goalkeepers, one of the best in post-war years being *Tommy Forgan* (1954-65). After leaving Hull, Forgan chalked up some 400 appearances with York. A later Bootham favourite was *Graeme Crawford,* who played in over 250 matches. Crawford began his League career with Sheffield United, and a number of other York goalkeepers have had links with Bramall Lane, including *Norman Wharton* and *Des Thompson.* One of Thompson's predecessors at Bootham was his father, George; and it is of interest to note that while with York, Des made a bit of football history in 1952 when he played against Scunthorpe United, for whom the goalkeeper was his brother George – the first time goalkeeping brothers had met in the League.

4. Full-Back Favourites

Ray Wilson and a Town tradition
One of the heroes of England's World Cup triumph of 1966, Ray Wilson, provides a classic example of Huddersfield Town's long line of great full-backs who include *Sam Wadsworth, Fred Bullock* and especially *Roy Goodall*, capped 25 times by England. Wilson (now, incidentally, an undertaker by trade) is often remembered as an old Evertonian, but he spent the first years of his career at Leeds Road, in that time making nearly 270 League appearances and gaining the first 24 of his 63 caps. The Shirebrook product joined the club's groundstaff in 1952, his breakthrough coming after his conversion from a wing-half into one of the game's most cultured left-backs.

In post-war years Town have produced many notable back partnerships, one of the best being that of Staniforth and Kelly. *Laurie Kelly* arrived from Wolves in 1950, *Ron Staniforth* from Stockport in 1952: they were everpresents in the promotion team of 1953 and for four years key figures in an excellent defence in a fine Town side. Then, after some 100 outings, Staniforth joined Sheffield Wednesday, helping the Owls win the Second Division title twice, while Kelly soldiered on to chalk up some 250 League appearances before quitting in 1956. Staniforth's classy play during his time at Leeds Road brought him eight England caps.

Subsequently Wilson emerged as one of Town's most exciting "finds". Then when he joined Everton, the accolade of fame as a home-produced back of quality fell upon local boy *Bob McNab*, who joined the club as an amateur in 1961 and turned professional in 1963. However, by the time he had made some 70 appearances he was one of the most sought-after defenders in the game, and in 1966 he was sold to Arsenal, the £50,000 fee being a record for a back.

Backs continued to help boost Huddersfield's finances. Other products of the 1960s included *Derek Parkin* and *Chris Cattlin,* but both made only some 60 appearances before they also attracted big offers which the club could not refuse. Parkin went to Wolves for £80,000, and Cattlin joined Coventry for £70,000, both moves being completed in early 1968.

*

George Hardwick, the Middlesbrough "Matinee Idol"
Tall, dark and handsome, George Hardwick was the Middlesbrough man with the matinee idol's looks, moustache and all: an outstanding and intelligent full-back who brought a dash of glamour and style to the game in the austere 1940s when he captained England in more than half of his 30-plus international appearances.

Laurie Scott, the Sheffield-born defender who partnered Hardwick in all but a handful of the Middlesbrough man's run of representative games between 1941 and 1948, told me: "George was a great player. He had it all: strength, speed, positional play and perception. He was very knowledgeable and could read a game so well that he was always one step ahead of the opposition; and his anticipation, speed over the first ten yards, and impeccable distribution skills made him a true master."

Roy Goodall, a prince of backs, played in the FA Cup finals of 1928 and 1930. Here he plays a snooker shot, watched by his Huddersfield colleagues Sid Binks and Bill Cook.

Saltburn-born Hardwick arrived at Ayresome Park in 1937 and made his League debut at 17 alongside the experienced George Laking (like Scott a Sheffield product). But for the war he would have made a lot more than some 150 League appearances for 'Boro. In the event, he was limited to 40 outings for the club between 1940 and 1946, and actually played twice as many times in those years as a guest with Chelsea, whom he helped to two wartime Wembley finals, including the League South Cup triumph of 1945.

After collecting 17 wartime caps, Hardwick added 13 more in the immediate post-war period during which he matured into an inspiring skipper; and in May 1947 he had the distinction of captaining the Great Britain side which scored a memorable 6-1 victory over the Rest of Europe at Hampden Park. Incidentally, in that game Hardwick played at right-back, but his usual role was on the left flank.

He left Middlesbrough in late 1950 when a £14,500 fee took him to Oldham as player-manager in that period when player-managers were fashionable following the success of Carter at Hull and Doherty at Doncaster. But Hardwick did not enjoy the managerial side of the job and soon reverted to being just a player until his retirement in 1956. Later, however, he had further spells as a manager, at Sunderland and Gateshead, but eventually he left the game – and football was the poorer for the loss.

It is often forgotten that in Hardwick's later years at Ayresome he had a back partner whom many thought might have joined him in the England side. But for the form of Scott, *Dick Robinson* would surely have gained the international recognition he deserved. As it was, Robinson's consolations were five Football League "caps" and the lasting appreciation and admiration of Ayresome regulars in a long and loyal career (1946-58) during which he made some 400 senior appearances.

After Hardwick's departure 'Boro fell into decline and dropped into the Second Division in 1954, and it was 20 years before they climbed back. In fact, they have had two spells in Division Three in the past 34 years, but now they're in the top grade again. Yet if they have had their lean times they have continued to produce fine backs. *Gordon Jones* (1960-73) emerged as a star at 17, gained England Under-23 recognition, and went on to make nearly 460 League appearances; while both *Mick McNeil* (1957-64) and *Cyril Knowles* (1962-64) emerged as England defenders, McNeil later playing with Ipswich, Knowles moving to Tottenham after only 37 League games for 'Boro. At the time of the 1974 promotion triumph, 'Boro were well served by a pair of backs widely admired in the game: *John Craggs* (1971-81), who made over 400 appearances; and *Frank Spraggon* (1963-75), who played in nearly 300 games.

Hull have been blessed with loyal defenders over the years, including Danish international *Vigo Jensen* (1948-56), whose 308 League appearances brought him 50 goals; and *Andy Davidson* (1949-67), the ex-Scottish junior who had a long wait for his chance but then (despite breaking a leg three times) went on to clock up 520 League appearances.

*

Loyal Men of Leeds

The line of Leeds United backs over the past 60 years includes nine who between them made nearly 4,000 appearances. That's an average of almost 450 games apiece, which serves to show how exceptionally well served the club has been in this department by performers whose keynote was loyalty and consistency. The list includes *Paul Madeley* and *Trevor Cherry* – and neither man was principally a back. Yet between them they filled the role in more than 300 matches, and it seems as appropriate to mention them here as anywhere else.

Madeley's 725 appearances between 1963 and 1981 saw him play in every position on the field except goalkeeper, and when first Reaney and then Cooper, the regular backs, each broke a leg, he was their replacement. Cooper's continued absence prompted United to pay £100,000 to Huddersfield for Cherry, and though he was nominally a defensive half-back he began at left-back and more than 200 of his 484 outings were at back. Both Madeley and Cherry were great team men (Cherry later became captain), and it was a measure of the regard in which they were held that they collected 35 caps between them, Cherry's quota being 27.

Paul Reaney (1962-77) and *Terry Cooper* (1963-74) were classic examples of the new breed of backs emerging as they began their careers. Backs became supplementary wingers as well as defenders, and Reaney and Cooper were fine exponents of "overlapping." Yet while they frequently joined in attacks and "made" many goals for others, in a joint tally of over 1,000 games they managed only 20 goals between them. However, it will not be forgotten that one of Cooper's goals won Leeds the 1968 League Cup final!

Reaney, London-born but raised in Yorkshire, played in nearly 750 matches at right-back and earned three caps. Injuries limited Cooper to 350 League and Cup games, but the Castleford product played 19 times for England; and though Reaney was just as sound and speedy, it was Cooper, operating on the left, who enjoyed the greater reputation as one of the game's best attacking backs. Cooper was later with Middlesbrough and, briefly, Doncaster; but in spells with both Bristol clubs he made history at Ashton Gate where he became football's first player-director.

Among earlier Leeds backs the *Milburn brothers* stood out: between them Jack (1927-39), George (1928-37) and Jim (1935-52) totted up nearly 800 peacetime appearances and some 120 in wartime; and Jack and George played together in some 150 matches. Those Ashington boys (uncles of Jack Charlton) were tough, firm and fearless. Jack, the oldest, played in some 400 games and his tally of 30 goals was a tribute to his prowess as a penalty-taker. George, at times overshadowed by his brother, was limited to 116 outings and managed only one goal; but when he moved to Chesterfield he proved himself as good with spot-kicks as Jack – and on one famous occasion in June 1947 converted three penalties against Sheffield Wednesday.

Jim, the youngest of the Milburn clan, had the longest wait for recognition, making only one senior appearance in his first five years at Elland Road. But he made up for it with over 50 games during the war and 220 between 1946 and 1952, from 1947 establishing a notable partnership with *Jimmy Dunn*, who arrived from Rotherglen just after United had been relegated to the Second Division.

There was a touch of irony in the fact that when Leeds went down in 1947 they were replaced in Division One by Manchester City, for City's right-back was the old United man, *Bert Sproston.* He had arrived at Elland Road from Sandbach in 1933, and though he didn't make an immediate impression, by 1935 he had displaced George Milburn and proved such a fine performer that by 1938 he had collected eight England caps. Alas, after some 140 games he was sold to Spurs during a period of financial stress at Leeds, and they soon had cause to regret it.

But eventually Dunn arrived from Scotland to plug the gap. For a time Dunn was chiefly associated with Jim Milburn, but later his name became synonymous with *Grenville Hair,* who came from Newhall United (Derbyshire) in 1948. Between them Dunn and Hair

Mick Whitham, one of Sheffield United's first internationals.

clocked up nearly 900 appearances. Dunn, who finished with a tally of 422, had played in some 140 games before Burton-born Hair started on his run of 474 matches; but the contrast in age and experience did not prevent them from becoming one of the game's best back partnerships, and they appeared together in more than 270 matches.

Reference to United backs reminds one of the many links between Elland Road and Bradford. Jim Milburn played about 100 times for Park Avenue before hanging up his boots, while brother Jack had spells as both player and manager over at Valley Parade. Later Paul Reaney and Trevor Cherry were also associated with Bradford City. Grenville Hair, after a period at Wellington, returned to West Yorkshire and became first trainer and then manager at Valley Parade. Sadly, just a few weeks after taking over as team-boss there, Hair collapsed and died during a training session.

The Bradford clubs have boasted many fine and loyal backs. In the 1950s, for instance, *Jeff Suddards* made some 343 appearances for Park Avenue; while *Tommy Flockett* totted up nearly 250 games for City. In more recent times both *Ian Cooper* (1965-76), with 442 League games, and *Cec Podd* (1970-83), with 494 games have assured themselves of a place in the Valley Parade hall of fame.

It might be appropriate here to mention another loyal back: *George Howe*, who was born at Wakefield and made 40 appearances with Huddersfield, but then went over to York City where he chalked up over 300 League outings between 1954 and 1960.

*

Some Sheffield and South Yorkshire Stalwarts
One of the greatest full-backs of the inter-war period was Sheffield Wednesday's *Ernest Blenkinsop* (1923-34), who played in 424 games and helped them win the Second Division title in 1926 and the League Championship in 1929 and 1930.

Blenkinsop's best-remembered partner at Hillsborough was Scot *Tommy Walker,* signed from Bradford City in 1926. However, by the time of the 1935 FA Cup triumph their era was over: "Blenkie" having gone to Liverpool, Walker having been dropped during the Wembley run. Walker's replacement from Aston Villa, *Joe Nibloe,* had previously helped Kilmarnock win the Scottish Cup, so the defeat of West Brom in the 1935 final enabled him to complete a rare double. *Ted Catlin,* a former Middlesbrough Boys' captain, had the unenviable task of stepping into Blenkinsop's boots, but he made such a success of it that he played in over 270 games and collected five England caps, surviving to play in the 1943 League North Cup final.

Barnsley's line of backs in the years from 1919 to 1939 extended from *Jimmy Spoors* to *Bob Shotton,* and included Gittins, Tindall, Williams, Everest and Sam Cookson, not forgetting Penistone product Herbert Hodgkinson, who was a great favourite in the 1920s.

During Barnsley's run to promotion in 1934, Shotton's partner, *Aneurin Richards* suffered a broken leg; then during the promotion campaign of 1938-39 Shotton himself fell victim to a serious injury. The latter setback prompted Barnsley to pay a substantial fee for Bradford City's *Gordon Pallister,* destined not only to become one of the most famous of Oakwell backs but later to serve the club for many years as a director.

Rotherham's most notable back in the 1930s was probably *Reg Freeman,* who had learned his trade with Northern Nomads and Oldham before joining Middlesbrough in 1923. He arrived at Millmoor in 1930 and in 1932 earned a novel place in the record books when he scored the first goal of his League career . . . in his 325th match!

As mentioned earlier, Freeman became player-manager and then manager at Rotherham. In the late 1940s he built a fine side which lifted the Third Division (North) title in 1951 after three near-misses; and in this period the back favourites were Doncaster-born *Jack Selkirk* and *Norman Noble,* who between them clocked up over 750 League appearances. Noble, the former Barnsley Boys captain, had been with Huddersfield and Bradford City before joining Rotherham to succeed Fred Hanson at left-back. Later Noble switched to centre-half and in 1955 had the misfortune to miss a last-match penalty when Rotherham were pipped for a place in the First Division on goal-average.

Another back in Noble's time was *Dennis Warner.* Later came local lads *Peter Johnson* and *Lol Morgan.* Johnson, a Rawmarsh product, played in over 150 games before his 1957 move to Sheffield Wednesday; while Morgan topped 300 matches. Rotherham have always been well served by backs, and *John Breckin* (1971-82) epitomised the tradition with over 400 League outings, while colleague *Gerry Forrest,* after some 300 games, later enjoyed success with Southampton.

Above: Barry Murphy, who made 550 appearances for Barnsley between 1962 and 1978.

Right: Ted Catlin, a former Middlesbrough Boys' captain, had the unenviable task of stepping into the boots of Ernest Blenkinsop.

Over at Barnsley, Pallister's career was interrupted by the war, but he played in over 100 wartime games and later brought his tally of peacetime appearances to some 240 and also played for the Football League XI. Other Oakwell backs have included *Arthur Glover, John Thomas, Harry May, Colin Swift* and *John Short*; and more recently three who passed into the record books were local products *Eric Brookes* (over 370 games, 1960-68) and *Phil Chambers* (450 matches, 1970-83), plus North Easterner *Barry Murphy*, whose tally of appearances between 1962 and 1978 topped 550.

Down the road at Doncaster, Irish international *Bill Graham* (1949-58) enjoyed a run of over 300 games during a colourful phase in Rovers' history.

Albert Cox had his first taste of senior soccer at the age of 18 in Sheffield United's 1936 Cup semi-final side. He went on to play in the first team on 87 occasions before the war, and between 1946 and 1951 he lifted his tally of appearances to nearly 300 in a period when his name became synonymous with that of *Fred Furniss*. Wartime discovery Furniss played in more than 120 games betwen 1941 and 1946 and afterwards chalked up over 300 senior outings. Furniss had the good fortune to step in when *Eddie Shimwell* fell foul of the United board because he took a public house. Shimwell moved to Blackpool, where he gained an England cap and played in the FA Cup finals of 1948, 1951 and 1953.

Cec Coldwell, successor to Furniss, was yet another local discovery, and what an excellent servant he proved to be between 1951 and 1966. In over 450 games Coldwell showed himself a sound and intelligent back. He had a spell as skipper in his latter years, then joined the training staff, and had a notable run as acting manager before quitting to become a newsagent.

Coldwell's left-back partner *Graham Shaw* was one of United's finest defenders, and after succeeding Cox he played in some 490 games and collected five England caps. Shaw's younger brother, Bernard, looked set to add more senior caps to the family locker, but ultimately had to be satisfied with Under-23 recognition. In some 150 United games he proved himself an effective back, and later served Wolves and Sheffield Wednesday.

Just as Graham Shaw's name was synonymous with Coldwell's, so Bernard's was long associated with *Len Badger,* the Carbrook product who also gained Under-23 honours but never the "full" cap he deserved. A splendid back of flair and skill, Badger totted up 500 appearances between 1962 and 1975, establishing a second notable partnership with *Ted Hemsley,* one of that diminishing breed of League footballers who also played county cricket.

Just as United's early post-war backs were local lads, so were those at Hillsborough: Thurnscoe product *Frank Westlake* and Sheffielder *Hugh Swift.* Originally a winger, Swift emerged as a fine back, famous for his well-timed sliding tackles. He and Westlake enjoyed one run of over 100 consecutive appearances together; and but for the broken jaw which prematurely ended his playing days, Swift might have gained more than England "B" recognition.

Swift's successor was a tenacious bundle of energy and enthusiasm, *Norman Curtis* (1950-60), who played in over 320 games. Curtis excelled as an emergency goalkeeper (in one game he saved two penalties!) but is best remembered for his method of powering home penalties at the end of a long dash upfield.

In the era of Curtis the back polish was provided by the elegant ex-Huddersfield man, *Ron Staniforth,* and after Staniforth came *Peter Johnson* from Rotherham; while on the left flank Curtis was succeeded by *Don Megson,* who went on to play in nearly 450 games, his partner from the mid-1960s being *Wilf Smith.*

More recently Wednesday's back positions have been filled by local lad *Mel Sterland* and Irish international *Nigel Worthington.* Sterland, who has gained Under-21 honours and been close to a senior cap, has emerged as a great favourite and a popular choice as captain. He and Worthington (a £125,000 buy from Notts County in 1984) like to join in attacks, and Sterland has been especially successful as a marksman since coming into the first-team in 1979: he has scored some spectacular goals with his famous forward bursts and has also managed several vital conversions from the penalty spot.

5. Parade of the Pivots

A Squad of Internationals

Centre-halves – always called pivots in the old days because they were invariably the king-pins of a team, the focal point of operations – came in all shapes and sizes but were mostly tall, commanding figures, at the heart of the defence but poised to provide the first vital link with the forwards. The introduction of the third-back game after the change in the off-side law in 1925 turned many positive pivots into simple stoppers, and the trend has continued so that today we talk not of centre-halves but centre-backs, and now they usually work in pairs, like policemen on night patrol. But the concept of the old-style attacking centre-half remains very popular with spectators, and we still delight in the sight of a man in the No. 5 shirt joining his front men and showing them the way to goal.

Jack Charlton (1950-73), who played 35 times for England between 1965 and 1970 and figured in the famous World Cup triumph of 1966, was essentially a modern centre-back, yet in some 770 games for Leeds United he registered 95 goals, and his half-dozen in internationals took him past the century mark. The fact is that most of these goals stemmed from corner-kicks and other "dead ball" situations, another aspect of tactical trends which make use of a defender's height and weight while, at least in the case of the centre-back, not encouraging free runs forward except in certain circumstances.

Over the years many clubs, usually during periods when goals were scarce, have tried the regular centre-half at centre-forward; but it's a ploy which does not always pay dividends, for few defenders can make the switch with success. The classic example of the stopper-turned-striker succeeding brilliantly was the legendary *John Charles* at Leeds. With over 150 goals to his name, Charles really belongs in the later chapter on goal-kings, but "the gentle giant" was first a great centre-half. Indeed, more than 150 of his 327 appearances for Leeds and 17 of his 38 games for Wales were in the No. 5 shirt. Charles missed Leeds United's peak years, and for all his fame at home and in Italy, he must have envied Jack Charlton, who played in seven Cup finals and won a League Championship medal.

Tony Leach (1926-34), who was capped twice by England in 1930 and made some 260 appearances with Sheffield Wednesday, was one of those lucky enough to collect two League Championship medals; but his good fortune was really in the way his career was transformed after manager Bob Brown converted him into a centre-half and created the famous middle line of Strange, Leach and Marsden.

Vincent Matthews, capped twice in 1928, was bigger and more rugged than some of his Sheffield United predecessors at centre-half in the England team (such as Morren and Wilkinson); but what was novel about his story was the way he suddenly emerged as an international candidate after his move from Tranmere Rovers. True enough, club prizes eluded him, but when United were knocked off the Wembley trail after the semi-final "marathon" of 1928, Matthews at least had the consolation of having been involved in an epic series which brought him to the attention of the media and selectors.

About the time Matthews was collecting his England caps, a tall, rangy Welshman, *Tom Griffiths,* was coming into international reckoning as successor to the legendary Fred Keenor. After spells with Everton and Bolton, Griffiths had a dozen of his 21 caps already won before he moved to Middlesbrough. Unfortunately, with all his clubs he was more often involved in relegation struggles than in chasing trophies; and when he left Ayresome in 1935 he was one of seven players signed by Aston Villa in a last-ditch attempt to avoid the fall into Division Two. But Villa went down . . . and 'Boro stayed up!

In the post-war era Yorkshire clubs have provided some notable Scottish international defenders, among them centre-halves *Gordon McQueen* and *Eddie Colquhoun.* McQueen, signed by Leeds from St. Mirren for £30,000 in 1972, gained 17 of his 30 caps while at Elland Road and was in the 1974 League Championship side. In 1978, after some 170 matches, he moved to Manchester United for £495,000 – at the time a record transfer fee between British clubs. Colquhoun cost Sheffield United a mere fraction of that when he came from West Brom

in 1968, but he proved just as good an investment. The tall Scot helped United regain their First Division place in 1971 and he went on to make 360 League appearances and collect nine caps.

Few of the men who have played at centre-half with Yorkshire clubs can equal the record of *Terry Neill,* who gained 59 caps for Northern Ireland. But all but 15 of these came before he joined Hull City in 1970. Neill, best remembered as the man who made over 250 appearances for Arsenal, played in some 100 matches for City. Other England internationals from the region have included *Tom Crawshaw, George Wilson* and *Peter Swan* (Wednesday), *Alf Young* (Huddersfield), *Ernie Hart* (Leeds) and *Frank Barson,* who began his career at Barnsley.

*

Loyal Men, Lasting Favourites

Defenders in general and pivots in particular tend to be among the most loyal; though, of course, long service and consistency don't necessarily mean a man will gain recognition

Left: *Sam Cowan, international centre-half who started with Doncaster Rovers.*
Centre: *Tom Giffiths, Middlesbrough's Welsh international.*
Right: *Ernest Hart (Leeds United).*

beyond his home area. Some of the most dependable players in the business have missed out on honours, and a few who deserved international recognition never got it.

Joe Shaw, who served Sheffield United from 1948 to 1966 and clocked up nearly 700 appearances, was a classic example of a player whose talents never brought him the England place he deserved. Shaw began his career as a wing-half or inside-forward, but the bulk of his 629 League matches were in the No. 5 shirt, and in his time he was rated as the game's finest uncapped player in that position. Joe Mercer, one of football's legendary figures and a former United manager, often said that Shaw was in a class of his own. "He made the job look so easy and always seemed to have time to take the lace out of the ball – the sure mark of a great player. What a shame he never won a cap." On the small side for a defender, Shaw was one of the great idols of Bramall Lane in the post-war era.

Sheffield United always had a tradition for producing home-grown, loyal and dependable performers, and notable among these were *Tom Johnson* and *Harry Latham.* Johnson was

Joe Shaw, a great centre half who went on to manage York City.

Tom Johnson (Sheffield United)

one of the trio of members of the famous Ecclesfield family which served United over a span of more than 50 years; and if his father and elder brother (both called Harry) enjoyed greater fame, Tom was highly rated and made over 250 appearances, playing in the 1936 FA Cup final side and the 1939 promotion team. Latham, who between 1940 and 1952 played in some 420 matches, was a stopper pure and simple, uncompromising and unpretentious but very effective. Latham epitomised the spirit and consistency of a United side which had no stars but still won the League North championship in 1946.

Wednesday's line of pivots has included a number of home-grown heroes, from *Frank Froggatt* and *Fred Kean* in the 1920s to *Mark Smith,* who made over 350 appearances between 1977 and 1987 and contributed to the climb from the Third to the First Division. A hero of the 'thirties was *Walt Millership,* so tough that they dubbed him "Battleship": he

"Battling Barson"

"Battling Barson" of Barnsley has passed into football folklore as one of the hardest defenders in soccer history, remembered as the most suspended player of his era. He mastered the arts of intimidation, retribution and survival at Oakwell from 1911 to 1919. He then moved to Aston Villa where he captained the club in its famous 1920 FA cup final victory over Huddersfield Town.

arrived from Bradford in 1930 and played in over 380 games, including the FA Cup final triumph of 1935. Millership's post-war successors included *Cyril Turton* and *Edgar Packard*. Turton (1943-54) made some 200 appearances and was said to be able to run faster backwards than forwards! Packard, though often kept out of the side by Turton, still managed some 150 games and is often remembered for the only League goal he ever scored – a brilliant solo effort at the end of a dribble almost the length of the field!

Vic Mobley was one of the unluckiest of Wednesday centre-halves. Injury cost him a place in the England side in 1965 when he had to withdraw from the match with Holland; and

a year later he was injured in the FA Cup semi-final and had to miss Wembley. Mobley's misfortune was a lucky break for *Sam Ellis,* who earned a place in the records because he made his Cup debut in that 1966 final. *Mick Lyons* was another centre-half who never collected the honours he deserved, but after his move to Hillsborough he became a great favourite and led Wednesday to promotion in 1984.

Long-serving centre-halves abound in the records of Yorkshire clubs, and the roll of honour includes York City's *Barry Jackson* (481 League games, 1958-69) and *Chris Topping* (402 League games, 1968-77); Halifax Town's *John Pickering* (400 games, 1965-74) and *Alex South* (302 League appearances, 1956-64); Hull City's *Tom Berry* (376 League matches, 1947-57); Huddersfield's *John Coddington* (332 League games, 1955-66); and Rotherham's *Peter Madden* (308 League matches, 1955-66). *Sid Bycroft,* who made 460 appearances between 1935 and 1951, was one of the many "characters" produced by Doncaster Rovers; and after him came another, *Charlie Williams* (1949-58), who has assured himself of a place in the mythology of Yorkshire football. Williams, who made over 160 appearances for Rovers, later earned fame as a comedian. In his club act he joked that he was never much of a footballer: "I couldn't play, really, but I was good at stopping those who could!"

Williams subsequently became a director of Barnsley, a club whose reputation for producing centre-halves included the discovery of *Frank Barson* and *Bernard Harper. George Henderson* and *Tom Holley* were other pre-war favourites: Henderson making some 250 appearances in the 1930s, Holley managing some 80 games before his move to Leeds. Tom later became a popular sports journalist.

In post-war years Barnsley's line of pivots has included the popular *Duncan Sharp* (1953-61), who totted up over 200 League outings; *Pat Howard* (180 games, 1965-71); and *Mick McCarthy* (290 matches, 1977-83). Sharp was a great favourite and in some eyes the best: but his successor, *Eric Winstanley* (1961-72), was the longer-lasting, for "Winnie" wrote his name into the club's records by chalking up over 450 appearances. Winstanley epitomised the kind of loyalty Barnsley always inspired in their local discoveries, and many felt that he might have earned fame beyond Oakwell had he moved on before he passed his peak. He saw colleague *Pat Howard* enjoy greater rewards at Newcastle United and Arsenal; while his successors *Mick Pickering* (100 League games, 1974-76) and *Mick McCarthy* tasted life at the top and the kind of success which eluded Winstanley. McCarthy, who moved to Manchester City, was as much a South Yorkshire "Tyke" as Winstanley, but he adapted easily to Scottish football with Celtic, and rule changes at international level enabled him to qualify for Eire, in whose national team he played alongside several other Englishmen, including ex-Wednesday back Chris Morris, under the management of England World Cup hero Jack Charlton.

An earlier Oakwell defender, *Barry Swallow*, merits attention, too. As the son of an old Barnsley and Doncaster back, he had spells with the Reds, Doncaster Rovers and Bradford City and clocked up some 220 League games before taking his final tally of appearances to around the 500 mark in a six-year spell at York City in the early 1970s.

A Millmoor No. 5 worthy of a mention is *Horace Williams* (1942-53), who played in some 330 games and was a member of that famous side of the late 1940s. More recently *Paul Stancliffe* made some 300 appearances for the Millers between 1976 and 1983, enjoying considerable success before joining Sheffield United to add another notable chapter to his career.

Since the war Huddersfield centre-halves have included *Don McEvoy*, who played in over 150 games before moving to Sheffield Wednesday in 1954; *Ken Taylor*, who totted up over 250 appearances between 1953 and

Don McEvoy, who played in over 150 games for Huddersfield Town.

1964 and spent his summers making runs for Yorkshire CCC; and *Roy Ellam*, who played in some 150 games for Bradford City before clocking up over 200 appearances for Town.

In the early post-war period Middlesbrough boasted an outstanding centre-half in *Bill Whitaker*, signed from Chesterfield in 1947 and going on to make some 190 appearances. *Dick Robinson*, mentioned previously as the back partner of George Hardwick, later gave fine service at centre-half; and other 'Boro men excelling in this role have included *Brian Phillips, Bill Gates, Dickie Rooks,* and *Stuart Boam;* while the present defensive king-pin, *Gary Pallister*, has gained England honours after being one of the heroes of the clubs's triumphant return to the First Division in 1988.

6. Wing-Halves and Inside-Forwards

When big fees were not so common!

The deal which took Bradford City midfielder *Stuart McCall* to Everton for £875,00 in the summer of 1988 provided yet another reminder that these days huge transfer fees are so commonplace as to prompt little comment. So it is difficult to imagine the sense of shock and outrage which greeted the first-ever four-figure deal back in 1905 when *Alf Common* moved from Sunderland to Middlesbrough for £1,000. The critics branded Common "the wandering Jew of football" and supporters everywhere predicted that money would ruin the game!

Common's sensational transfer certainly created an outcry at Bramall Lane, for only a few months before his switch to Ayresome Park, Common had been sold to Sunderland by Sheffield United for £520. United were not simply upset that Sunderland had made a quick profit: they had declined several better offers for Common because the player had insisted that Sunderland was the only club for which he wished to play.

It was from the Roker club that United had signed him in the first place, for £350 in 1901. Within a few months Common had helped the Blades win the FA Cup and by 1904 had gained the first of his three England caps. United were disappointed to lose their star, and by coincidence news of his unexpected move to Middlesbrough came on the eve of 'Boro's visit to Bramall Lane. At the time 'Boro were struggling to avoid relegation and hadn't won an away game for nearly two years. Just to add insult to injury they defeated United – and Common got the winning goal from the penalty spot!

When people talk of ball artists the name most often quoted is that of *Len Shackleton*, the Bradford product who was dubbed "the Clown Prince of Soccer" because his extraordinary skills made him such a great entertainer. Perhaps he was too much of an individualist in some eyes, for the selectors called him into the England side only five times.

It was after a year at Arsenal, where he was told he would never make the grade, that Shackleton returned to Yorkshire in 1940 and joined Bradford PA. In the war years he played in over 200 games and scored 160 goals for Park Avenue and occasionally guested for other clubs: indeed, on Christmas Day 1940 he played for Park Avenue in the morning and for Bradford City in the afternoon! Such was his progress that it was no surprise when Newcastle paid £13,000 for him in late 1946, and soon after his arrival on Tyneside he scored six goals in one game. Then in February 1948 he became the game's costliest footballer when Sunderland spent £20,050 to buy him.

The accolade of Britain's most expensive player passed to another inside-forward, *Jackie Sewell*, in March 1951 when Sheffield Wednesday paid Notts County £35,000. Sewell became a big favourite at Hillsborough, making 175 appearances and scoring 92 goals before his move to Aston Villa in 1955. He helped the Owls win two Second Division titles and collected six caps, concluding his League career with some 50 outings for Hull City.

It is intriguing to note that Wednesday only signed Sewell because they failed to persuade Sheffield United idol Jimmy Hagan to move across the city after a £32,000 deal had been agreed. It is also of interest to recall that Wednesday let Sewell go because of the outstanding form of two locally-produced inside men who had cost them only £10 apiece – *Redfern Froggatt* and *Albert Quixall*. Froggatt (like his father before him) captained Wednesday to a Second Division title triumph; and with 149 goals in 458 games he was recognised as one of the club's most loyal and consistent players. Quixall, with five caps, won one more than Froggatt, and he earned greater fame because in September 1958 he became Britain's costliest footballer when Matt Busby paid £45,000 to take him to Manchester United. Quixall made some 260 appearances for Wednesday and, with his blond hair, boyish looks and brief shorts, was the darling of the crowd.

When Quixall helped Manchester United win the FA Cup in 1963 his fellow inside-forward was another blond hero with Yorkshire connections, the legendary *Denis Law*, who had the distinction of being a record fee man three times. Law emerged as one of the greatest players of his era, collecting 55 Scottish caps and scoring over 200 League goals. Yet when he arrived at Huddersfield Town to join the groundstaff in 1955 he was a pale slip of a boy in spectacles. Town's manager Andy Beattie had recruited him on the recommendation of his brother, Bob, and at first sight he wondered whether Bob wasn't playing some sort of joke on him. But when Law went onto the field it was soon obvious that he had special qualities. At 16 he was given his first taste of League soccer, and after some 80 games he was able to command a record fee of £53,000 when he was sold to Manchester City in 1960. A year later he moved to Torino for £100,000, but Italian fare didn't suit him and in 1962 he joined Manchester United. The fee United paid, £116,000, doesn't seem much by modern standards, but had the deal occurred 25 years later you can bet the figures would have been ten times as high – and Law would still have been a bargain at the price!

*

Alf Common, who became soccer's first four-figure transfer when he moved from Sunderland to Middlesbrough for £1,000 in 1905.

Four of the Best

At one stage in the late 1940s and early 1950s four of the greatest inside-forwards in the history of football were all playing with Yorkshire clubs: *Raich Carter* was player-manager at Hull City; *Peter Doherty* had three years with Huddersfield Town and then became player-manager at Doncaster Rovers; *Jimmy Hagan* was winning the praises of all but the England selectors at Sheffield United; and *Wilf Mannion* was making magic at Middlesbrough.

Three of the four were products of the North East, while Doherty hailed from a part

Sheffield United, 1952. Back row: Joe Shaw, Fred Furniss, Ted Burgin, Howard Johnson, Colin Rawson, Graham Shaw. Front row: Alf Ringstead, Jimmy Hagan, Len Browning, Harold Brook, Derek Hawksworth. Several members of the team also played for other clubs – Burgin for Doncaster and Leeds, Rawson for Rotherham, Browning and Brook for Leeds, and Hawksworth for Huddersfield and Bradford City.

of Ireland well-known for breeding fine footballers. All had in common superb ball skills, tactical flair, the will to win and the total mastery of canny craftsmen who were always one step ahead of the game. Schemers they were, but they knew that goals counted; and while Carter and Doherty each bagged over 200 in more than 400 games, Hagan and Mannion both topped the century mark.

Surprisingly, between them they collected only 56 caps in peacetime, for they lost some good years to the war; and we should remember that anyway there were fewer international matches in their day. But also they were often neglected by the selectors; and none more so than Hagan, who made 16 wartime appearances but played for England only once afterwards.

Of the four, Carter and Doherty were the only ones to capture major club honours, Carter helping Sunderland win the League Championship in 1936 and the FA Cup in 1937, Doherty playing in Manchester City's League

Championship side of 1937; and the pair playing together in Derby County's 1946 FA Cup-winning team. Later Carter led Hull to the Third Division (North) title in 1949, and Doherty did the same with Doncaster a year later. Hagan helped Sheffield United win promotion in 1939 and the Second Division title in 1953, but Mannion's team found the honours elusive.

Carter and Mannion have often been described by former colleagues as the greatest players they ever knew, "complete" footballers, precise, perceptive and powerful influences. Carter, who collected 13 caps and played in 17 wartime internationals, moved to Yorkshire in 1948 as the first of a new breed of player-managers, and if some felt his best days were behind him he proved that a wise old head is a match for most as he led Hull to success. As long as the silver-haired Carter could play he seemed able to guarantee the right results more often than not: only later, when his fate was in the hands of others, did he experience mixed fortunes as manager of Leeds and Middlesbrough.

At Ayresome Park he might have done better if the team had had a Mannion. But Mannion, so long the Middlesbrough maestro, had gone. Mannion was unfortunate in that his League career ended too soon in sad circumstances. Following in a line of 'Boro inside-forward favourites, which included Jimmy Carr, Billy Birrell and the pint-sized Benny Yorston, Mannion eclipsed them all and between 1937 and 1953 made over 350 appearances, playing 30 times for England (including four wartime games) and figuring in the Great Britain team which crushed the Rest of Europe in 1947. But, fighting for a better deal in the era of the £12-a-week footballer, he created problems for himself, and at one stage he chose to quit the game but then returned to join Hull for a £5,000 fee in 1954. Unfortunately, during his brief retirement he had made some startling revelations in a newspaper, which brought him an instant FA ban, and by the time it was lifted his career had pushed him into obscurity.

Today when we think of the Mannion era, many remember not just the master but some of his colleauges, and especially *Micky Fenton*, the epitome of the Middlesbrough brand of loyalty. Fenton, an inside or centre-forward, managed only one England cap and never enjoyed the same adulation as Mannion; but the fact that he played in over 250 League games between 1934 and 1951 and, including wartime games, scored more than 200 goals serves to emphasise his value to the side.

Hagan, one of the greatest idols in Sheffield United's history, joined them in late 1938 from Derby for £2,500 and went on to make some 430 appearances and score 126 goals in the next 20 years. In fact, he played his early games on the wing and shared the limelight with several forward colleagues, including local lad *Jack Pickering*, who was capped once by England and played in over 360 games and scored over 100 goals for United between 1926 and 1948. Hagan's years in the army playing alongside internationals at Aldershot helped him mature

Left: *Raich Carter, player-manager of Hull and manager of Leeds United and Middlesbrough.*

Right: *Peter Doherty, a Huddersfield hero and later player-manager of Doncaster Rovers.*

into a master craftsman by the time he returned to Sheffield; and if the post-war period was a lean one for the Blades, their lack of success was hardly excuse for Hagan's continued absence from the national side.

Hagan was so often the golden star of the Sheffield scene and such a treasure that, in 1951, Wednesday were ready to break the British transfer record to take him to Hillsborough. But Hagan refused to go, and that is only one reason why supporters still remember him with great affection. True enough, in more

Tony Currie, who joined Leeds United for £240,000 in 1976.

recent times there have been those ready to suggest that *Tony Currie* was a better player, but whether this is so we shall never know – though how pleasant an exercise it is to try to reach a conclusion by imagining them playing in the same team! Currie, who cost United only £27,500 when he came from Watford in 1968, went on to make over 300 appearances before he left to join Leeds for £240,000 in 1976; and he played 17 times for England. Hagan's former team-mate Harold Brook once told me that Currie was Hagan's equal in ball skills and was better with his head; but I hesitate to reach a final verdict and am content to thank them both for many hours of pleasure.

Just before Hagan joined United they had another inside-forward of outstanding ability, *Bob Barclay*. Like Hagan, he arrived via Derby and between 1931 and 1937 made over 230 appearances and scored some 70 goals. Known as "the Alex James of Bramall Lane", Barclay collected three England caps. He moved to Huddersfield for a large fee, and with Town in 1938 played in his second FA Cup final (the first was with United in 1936). By the time the war was over Barclay had been succeeded at Huddersfield by Doherty, who arrived there after spells with Glentoran, Blackpool, Manchester City and Derby, and between 1946 and 1949 played in some 80 League games and scored over 30 goals for Town. Then Doherty joined Doncaster Rovers and as player-manager clocked up some 100 games and more than 50 goals before hanging up his boots in 1953.

As a non-playing manager he made a few notable discoveries and enjoyed some success, but the job was never as much fun as it had been before. People like Doherty (and Carter, Hagan and Mannion) found true fulfilment in playing, and it was as players that they gave football supporters the maximum pleasure. If only they didn't have to grow old!

*

Stars and Stalwarts

Many other wing-halves and inside-forwards have given pleasure to Yorkshire football followers down the years – indeed, almost too many to do justice to them all in the available space. The crowd's heroes – be they defensive half-backs, creative midfielders, "hard" men or shooting stars – are not confined to those with caps and medals and touched by fame.

Not that we can fail to note the internationals, for though merit does not always bring success or recognition, it is fair to say that those who have impressed the selectors have seldom been without merit even if you cannot always measure a man's popularity or prowess by the number of his caps.

Johnny Giles played 60 times for Eire and in some 520 outings for Leeds between 1963 and

WING-HALVES AND INSIDE-FORWARDS

1975 was idolised at Elland Road, his midfield partnership with Billy Bremner hailed as among the greatest; yet though his colleague Terry Yorath was capped 59 times by Wales, in 186 games for Leeds he was often the butt of the boo-boys, criticised for a lack of pace – as if he could be blamed for not being as gifted as some of his more illustrious colleagues!

Leeds' internationals have included the pint-sized Welshman *Brian Flynn*; the loyal and big-hearted Irishman, ex-'Boro man *Jim McCabe*; and *Wilbur Cush*, who played 14 times for Northern Ireland while with United. Two outstanding home crowd-pleasers were *Wilf Copping* and *Norman Hunter*, who passed into football folklore as the hardest tacklers of their time. Copping, capped 20 times by England in the 1930s, made over 180 appearances for Leeds before helping Arsenal win two League Championships and the FA Cup; and, an iron-man in the true traditions of his native Barnsley, he never shaved before a game to emphasise his mean and menacing look! Hunter managed over 700 games for Leeds between 1962 and 1976, collected 28 caps, and built a reputation for going where angels feared to tread: a ball-winner who didn't really bite opponents' legs (as supporters claimed) but made an effective and vital contribution to United's success in the Revie era.

Less fortunate hero of Leeds (and a much more creative player) was the brilliant but ill-fated *Eric Stephenson*, who was capped twice by England just before the war but then met his death while on active service with the Gurkha Rifles in Burma.

The club has been well served by men who never gained wider recognition: like the ever-dependable *Eric Kerfoot* (1949-59), who made nearly 350 appearances and had a spell as captain; and *Tommy Burden* (1948-54), with some 240 games.

Ken Willingham, ex Sheffield schoolboy star who played for Huddersfield and England.

Huddersfield Town have had many fine midfield men. Their line of international wing-halves includes Englishmen *Ken Willingham* (12 caps) and *Bill McGarry* (4), Scot *David Steele* (3) and former Irish boy star *Jimmy Nicholson* (1964-73), who gained 30 of his 40 caps after moving from Manchester United. McGarry (1951-60), sound if unspectacular, totted up some 400 appearances, while Nicholson's tally was around 300: classic examples of typical club loyalty. Some of Town's finest servants never won honours: men like *Eddie Boot*, the old Sheffield United man, over 300 games between 1937 and 1951; and *Len Quested*, over 200 outings in the early 1950s.

Town inside-forwards of note include *Les Massie* (334 League games, 98 goals), *Steve Smith* (329), *Jimmy Lawson* (234), *Jimmy Watson* (140), *Alan Gowling* and *Willie Davie*; plus some who also served other Yorkshire clubs, like *Albert Nightingale* (Sheffield United and Leeds), *Tommy Cavanagh* (Doncaster Rovers) and *Les Chapman* (Bradford City). Massie, of course, concluded his career at Halifax and Bradford PA; Lawson started at Middlesbrough and finished at Halifax; and The Shay was also the last stopping place for *Jimmy McGill*, who made some 160 appearances for Huddersfield and over 150 for Hull City.

The Huddersfield-Halifax link reminds us that *Willie Watson* began his career at Leeds Road and was later player-manager at The Shay. Watson's best years were spent at Sunderland, but he is remembered as the Yorkshireman who played for England at soccer and cricket in the 1950s. *Chris Balderstone* was another Huddersfield footballer who excelled at first-class cricket; though he, too, passed his best soccer years in "exile" at Carlisle after some 100 outings with Town. When he joined Doncaster Rovers in 1972 he made a piece of

sporting history: after batting for Leicestershire at Chesterfield during the day, he played for Rovers the same evening, returning to the wicket the following morning to complete a century!

We often think of wing-halves in pairs, and at Sheffield Wednesday certain names are synonymous: *Alf Strange* and *Billy Marsden*, *Wilf Sharp* and *Horace Burrows*, *Eddie Gannon* and *Doug Witcomb*, *Tom McAnearney* and *Tony Kay*, and *Peter Eustace* and *Gerry Young*. Strange gained 20 England caps (he once asked Mussolini for his autograph before a game in Italy!), but Marsden was limited to three, and his career ended abruptly when he suffered a spinal injury in a collision with colleague Roy Goodall (Huddersfield) while playing for England in Germany in 1930. Burrows was one of the classiest and most consistent half-backs of his day, making over 260 appearances and winning three caps before handing over to Joe Cockroft. After the war internationals Gannon (Eire) and Witcomb (Wales) each chalked up over 200 outings; but the McAnearney-Kay partnership of the late 1950s was hailed as the best since Strange and Marsden. McAnearney made over 380 appearances before being succeeded by the elegant Eustace, and, like Young later, was a great servant; but it was the fiery red-haired Kay who caught the eye, and in 1962 – before being capped – he became the game's costliest wing-half at £55,000 when Everton bought him. Sadly, Kay's career ended prematurely when he was banned by the FA following the betting coup scandal of 1964.

In the 1930s Wednesday had several brilliant inside-men, including England internationals *Ronnie Starling* (who started with Hull) and *Harry Burgess*. After their fall into Division Two in 1937 Wednesday recruited the

Opposite left: Ronnie Starling, once of Hull City later captain of Sheffield Wednesday.
Right: Jack Bestall, who started his football career at Rotherham.

clever Scot, *Charlie Napier*, known as "Happy Feet". In fact, Napier's international days were behind him when he arrived, and Wednesday had to wait 30 years until the arrival of *Jim McCalliog* to produce another capped Scottish inside-forward. McCalliog earned a place in the records when he joined Wednesday in 1965, for at £37,500 he was then the game's most expensive teenager. In 1969 another Scot, 18-year-old *Tommy Craig*, arrived from Aberdeen to become the club's first £100,000 player.

Among the "hard" men of the inter-war period Sheffield United's *Harold Pantling* ranked among the toughest, though he seems

Jack Sewell (Hull and Sheffield Wednesday)

to have had a sense of humour, too. After clogging a Bolton man in one match he saw the referee approaching and promptly raised his hands: "Okay, ref, I know I've done wrong. I'm going!" And off the field he walked! Pantling played in some 250 games for United, but gained only one England cap. His colleague in the 1925 Cup-winning team, *George Green*, was equally robust but also boasted superb ball skills, which earned him eight England caps. Green, who made over 420 appearances, is best remembered as part of the famous left-wing triangle which featured Gillespie and Tunstall. United "ball winners" of note in more recent times have included Scottish international *Alex Forbes* and Bradford born Welsh

international *Trevor Hockey*; while other long-serving half-backs of high talent include *Ernest Jackson* (some 360 games, 1935-49), and *Brian Richardson* and *Gerry Summers*, who together chalked up around 630 appearances.

Several United inside-forwards have had links with York: *Colin Addison*, who arrived via Nottingham Forest and Arsenal, started at Bootham in the late 1950s; while it was from United that City signed *Arthur Bottom*, who managed 90 goals in some 140 League games at York and was a hero of that famous 1955 run to the FA Cup semi-final. *Peter Wragg* also went via Bramall Lane to York and played over 260 times for City, but actually started at Rotherham and finished with Bradford City.

York have had many fine servants, and two who shone in that fine team of the mid-1950s were *Sid Storey* (over 350 games) and *Ron Spence* (300).

Irish international *Eric McMordie* finished his playing days at Bootham in the mid-1970s, but he is most readily associated with Middlesbrough, for whom he played more than 250 times. At Ayresome he followed in a line of outstanding inside-forwards, including the likes of Eire international *Arthur Fitzsimmons* (1949-59), who made over 250 appearances and scored some 50 goals for 'Boro. That fine 'Boro side of the 1920s included England half-back *Joe Peacock*; while in the 1950s *Bill Harris* arrived from Hull to collect six Welsh caps and chalk up nearly 400 appearances, and his contemporaries included such loyal men as *Jimmy Gordon, Harry Bell* and the versatile *Ronnie Dicks*. Later *Ron Yeomans* proved another fine servant. As midfielders go, the current idol of Ayresome is *Gary Hamilton*, the Glaswegian who has totted up 200 League appearances and been a key figure in the club's climb from the Third to the First Division in the late 1980s.

Among the loyal men of Barnsley *Charlie Baines*, the left-half who made some 340 League and Cup appearances between 1921 and 1930, merits a special place; and the most famous of modern wing-half products of Oak-

Old Harry Johnson (centre) was a great Bramall Lane favourite in the famous Sheffield United team of the 1890s. His son Harry (right) was a goal-king of the 1920s, and his other son, Tom, was a centre-half in United's 1936 F.A. Cup Final side. The Johnsons all came from Ecclesfield.

well was *Danny Blanchflower*, who began his great run as an Irish international while at Barnsley before moving via Aston Villa to become a member of that wonderful Tottenham side of the early 1960s.

Thanks to the writings of Michael Parkinson, *Sid "Skinner" Normanton*, one of Blanchflower's contemporaries, has passed into folklore as a legendary "hard" man in the Copping mould; but *Bob Glendenning*, who made 167 League and Cup appearances in the famous Barnsley side of the pre-1914 era, was probably much tougher. Over the years Barnsley have been well served by many equally effec-

tive and often more skilful players, among them *Henry Walters*, *John Bettany*, *Bobby Doyle* and *Alastair Millar*; and we should not forget the brilliant *Jimmy Baxter* from the 1940s and the 350-game *Bob Wood* (1951-64).

Rotherham have always been well-blessed with loyal and dependable half-backs and inside men, amongst them *Danny Williams* (620 games), *Gladstone Guest* (370), *Roy Lambert* (320) and *Jack Edwards* (300); and any reference to Millmoor has to include mention of *Albert Bennett*, *Brian Jackson*, *Frank Casper* and *David Bentley*. *Keith Kettleborough*, who started with Rotherham, later played with

Sheffield United and had a spell as Doncaster's player-manager.

Doncaster had one of the most loyal inside-men in the region in the early post-war era:

Ken Houghton (Rotherham and Hull).

Bert Tindill, who made over 400 appearances and scored some 130 goals and later played in 100 games for Barnsley. It is worthy of note that in more recent times Rovers produced the Snodin brothers, and *Ian Snodin*, after a spell at Leeds, went to Everton for £480,000 – though by 1988 his Goodison prospects seemed less promising following the transfer of £875,000 Stuart McCall from Bradford City.

Earlier reference to Rotherham reminds us that *Ken Houghton* made over 150 appearances with the Millmoor club before giving excellent service to Hull. Between 1964 and 1972 Houghton played over 250 games for City and lifted his tally of League goals to nearly 140.

His Hull predecessors include *Sid Gerrie* (1950-56) and *Ray Henderson* (1961-67), plus long-serving wing-halves in *Dennis Durham, Les Collinson, Brian Garvey* and *Malcolm Lord*. Rotherham were well served by *John Quinn*, who arrived from Sheffield Wednesday in 1967; and Quinn is also remembered with affection at Halifax, where other heroes have included such as *Bill Atkins, Tom Murphy* and *Stan Lonsdale*.

The Bradford clubs have also been handsomely served, City's loyal favourites including *Bruce Stowell* (over 400 games, 1959-71) and *Bob Webb*; while *Rod Johnson* concluded his career with some 200 matches for City in the 1970s after earlier spells with Leeds, Doncaster and Rotherham. Among those who have played for both Bradford clubs are *Whelan Ward* and *Bobby Ham*. Ward made over 150 appearances for City between 1948 and 1954 and then played some 100 times for Park Avenue. Ham began his career at Park Avenue around 1961 and made over 160 appearances; and, with spells at Preston and Rotherham in between, had two periods at Valley Parade, playing some 200 times for City and bringing his haul of goals for the Bradford clubs to over 120.

Terry Dolan also played with both Bradford clubs, starting with the ill-fated Park Avenue and then, after some five years at Huddersfield, chalking up around 200 games for Bradford City. Later he became manager at Bradford City and in 1988 piloted the club desperately close to what would have been a sensational return to the First Division.

7. Wizards of the Wing

Some Star Wingers

Wingers are the men who delight the crowds by creating excitement, usually with dazzling dribbles or dramatic dashes down the flanks. Sometimes they are essentially goal-makers, tricky performers who delight in throwing defences into disarray and creating openings for colleagues with flashes of brilliance or bursts of speed followed by pin-point crosses into the heart of the opposition's goalmouth. Sometimes they not only make chances but provide the finish themselves; and there is nothing quite as thrilling as a goal-scoring winger. But whether the wizard of the wing makes or takes the goals, so long as he is turning on the style he is assured of a special place in the affections of spectators.

Over the years Yorkshire clubs have produced some of the finest exponents of wing-play of all varieties, and it is a tradition which has been maintained in the county ever since the teenaged *Willie Mosforth* was the sensation of the 1880s when his wonderful long dribbles made him the idol of Olive Grove and at 19 Sheffield's youngest international. Mosforth's fame was later matched by *Fred Spiksley* in the 1890s.

In modern times when we think of a pair of wingers with contrasting but complimentary styles, men who stirred the blood with the ball skills of one and the lethal marksmanship of the other, we probably remember Scots *Peter Lorimer* and *Eddie Gray*, who played such a vital part in Leeds United's success in the Revie era. Together they registered nearly 1,300 appearances for the club between 1962 and 1986. Lorimer, who made his debut at 15, was the right-sided "goal kid" with dynamite in his boots, and he claimed a club record 237 goals – his 168 in the League being 15 more than the legendary John Charles managed. That Lorimer gained 21 caps to Gray's 12 and scored nearly four times as many goals does not mean he was the better player. On the contrary, Gray was in a class of his own, one of the most skilful footballers ever to wear a United shirt. Some of his performances were simply breathtaking, stunning in their brilliance; and thanks to television several of his greatest displays of mesmerising magic are preserved on film for posterity to enjoy. (Gray had a spell as United's player-manager, and in 1988, after a period in Lancashire, returned to Yorkshire to take charge at Hull City. May he yet prove as good a manager as he was a player!)

Lorimer and Gray were neither the first nor the last of United's international wingers. In fact, the first was an Irishman, *David Cochrane* (1937-51), who made some 180 appearances and whose dribbling skills, though perhaps never as great as Gray's, earned him 12 caps. After him came the 5ft 4ins Welshman *Harold Williams* (1949-56), capped twice during a United career which spanned some 220 games; and more recently *Carl Harris*, with 24 caps, joined the ranks of the club's Welsh internationals. *Arthur Graham*, with 260 appearances and 47 goals for Leeds, collected ten Scottish caps before his move to Manchester United in 1983.

Leeds have yet to produce an England winger, though they have had a couple of former internationals. There was, for instance, *Colin Grainger*, the singing outside-left, who gained six of his seven caps while with Sheffield Uni-

Fred Spikesley, Wednesday's wizard of the wing.

ted and joined Leeds in 1960 from Sunderland. Then there was *Bobby Turnbull* (1925-32), who played in over 200 games and scored some 50 goals for Leeds. This brilliant outside-right gained his only England cap while with Bradford PA, and it was there in 1918 that he shot himself into the record books by scoring five goals for Park Avenue against Barnsley – on his debut! Few wingers have done better than that in a single match at any stage in their careers, though *David Mercer* once hit six for Hull City against Sheffield United in 1919; and *Albert Turner* scored five for Doncaster Rovers against New Brighton in 1935 when his season's tally of 25 goals helped shoot the Belle Vue side to the Third Division (North) championship.

Reference to Turnbull prompts mention of two other England wingers who came to the fore at Bradford – *Jim Conlin* at Valley Parade more than 80 years ago; and *Albert Geldhard*, Park Avenue's "boy wonder" of the late 1920s. Durham-product Conlin, a diminutive outside-left, gained his only cap in 1906 and was promptly sold to Manchester City. Geldhard, who earned a unique place in the record books in 1929 when he made his League debut at the age of 15, was sold to Everton at 18, and it was at Goodison that he collected his four England caps. Incidentally, in the 1930s a famous ex-England winger, *Joe Spence*, arrived at Valley Parade from Manchester United and did City proud for two years before concluding his career at Chesterfield.

After all the Cup success they enjoyed in the late Victorian era, Sheffield United won the coveted trophy only twice afterwards, in 1915 and 1925; and in 1925 their team included two of Bramall Lane's greatest wingers, *David Mercer* and *Freddie Tunstall*. The pair joined United within the space of ten days in late 1920, Mercer costing £4,500 from Hull City, Tunstall £1,000 from Midland League Scunthorpe. Mercer's haul of 23 goals in some 240 games indicates that his role was changed from taker to maker after his move from Hull; but that he succeeded was confirmed by his selection to play for England twice in the early 1920s. Tunstall was always regarded as rather special: his link up with Green and Gillespie gave United one of the strongest left-flanks in the League. The Low Valley lad had one of the hardest shots in the game and claimed 135 goals in some 470 outings. He played seven times for England, but his proudest day came in that 1925 Cup final when he scored the winning goal – and did it using his "wrong" foot!

It was noted earlier that in *Colin Grainger* Sheffield United had an England winger who also made his name as a professional singer. Back in the 1930s Wednesday had a brilliant outside-left who appeared on stage as a concert pianist. *Ellis Rimmer* certainly hit the right notes on the field! In some 420 games between

1928 and 1938 he scored 140 goals for the Owls. He found the net in every round of the 1935 Cup run and scored twice in the Wembley defeat of West Brom, his goals coming at a time when the match seemed to be slipping from Wednesday's grasp. Rimmer was capped four times by England while his outside-right colleague, little *Mark Hooper*, never found favour with the selectors. Yet Hooper and Rimmer were among the best club wingers in the game, a wonderful pair together; and Hooper, who scored 136 goals in some 420 matches, was just as effective as his pal and equally deserving of representative honours.

In rounding up Sheffield's capped wingers mention should be made of *Alf Ringstead*, who had never seen a Football League match until he played in one after joining United in 1950. He went on to make some 260 appearances and score over 100 goals in the next ten years, and his talents earned him 20 games for Eire. When the Ringstead era ended, the arrival of John Harris as manager saw *Len Allchurch* brought from Swansea to fill the gap. Allchurch took his tally of Welsh caps to 11 in his time at Bramall Lane, but more significantly he arrived in time to make a vital contribution to United's successful promotion push of 1961. Four years later Harris clinched another Welsh bargain when he snapped up *Gil Reece* from Newport for £10,000. Reece went on to play 29 times for Wales, and in over 200 games for United his haul of more than 60 goals included some of the finest solo efforts ever seen at Bramall Lane.

Talking of brilliant solo goals reminds me that *George Robertson* (1909-20) was the only Wednesday winger to gain Scottish international honours while at Hillsborough. In his time the ex-Motherwell man enjoyed immense popularity for the way he set up goals for the likes of McLean and Wilson. However, if you asked a modern supporter to name his favourite Scottish winger he would promptly choose little *Willie Henderson*. Though Henderson's illustrious international career was over before his move to Sheffield, and though he stayed at the club only briefly after his arrival in 1972, he produced such tremendously entertaining skills that he became one of the greatest Hillsborough heroes of the decade.

In Huddersfield's golden age between the wars they were blessed with the services of two of the greatest wingers of the period: *Alex Jackson* and *Billy Smith*. It was a mark of Huddersfield's prowess in that era that they had five men on duty in the 1928 England-Scotland match. Jackson was the only one in the Scottish side, and he outshone his clubmates by grabbing a hat-trick in a memorable Scotland victory. As well as starring in 18 internationals Jackson was one of the most consistently brilliant club players in the game, a true genius. However, even he could not match the record of Billy Smith (1914-34), who played in well over 500 games for Town and helped them complete a League title treble as well as playing in three FA Cup finals. But for suspension Smith would have played in the 1920 final, but he made amends in 1922 by earning and then converting the penalty kick which gave Town the Cup. If Smith managed only three England caps he helped make a lot of Yorkshire soccer history; and he also earned a special personal niche in the record books when, in 1924, fol-

Billy Smith (Huddersfield).

lowing a rule change, he became the first man to score a goal direct from a corner-kick in a League match.

If Smith was limited to three FA Cup final appearances, one of his successors in the Town team made history by appearing in five. However, *Joe Hulme's* record included four Wembley visits with Arsenal, and it was only in 1938 that he went there with Huddersfield. In his time Hulme was regarded as the fastest footballer in Britain, and it is often forgotten that though he was born in Stafford he grew up in Yorkshire and began his professional career with York City. A fine cricketer, incidentally, he played with Middlesex and during the war guested in the Bradford League.

In the post-war era one of Town's most popular wingers was *Vic Metcalfe*, who played in some 500 games and scored over 100 goals between 1940 and 1958. Metcalfe was one of the best outside-lefts in the game and deserved more than the two caps he received. His Irish colleague *John McKenna* (1948-52) at least managed nine caps as an outside-right. In a later era *Mike O'Grady* claimed Metcalfe's old position and made over 160 appearances for Town before going to Leeds. O'Grady was very highly rated, but he, too, managed only two England caps.

Middlesbrough's earliest wing internationals were both outside-rights and both played for England. *Fred Pentland*, capped five times before the Great War, was described as one of the fastest players of his era; but *Bill Pease*, who played for 'Boro from 1926 to 1932, was not only fast but a prolific marksman. In his time at Ayresome he topped a century of goals, enjoying two of his best seasons in 1926-7 and 1928-9 when 'Boro won the Second Division championship. Pease actually played rugby at school and did not take up soccer until he joined the army; but he was good enough at an early stage to play as an amateur with Leeds City, and the astute Herbert Chapman soon took him to Northampton – so that he cost 'Boro a fee when they brought him back to Yorkshire! *Jack Carr*, incidentally, made the first of

his two England appearances at inside-right in 1920 when he partnered Bradford's *Bobby Turnbull*; but his second cap in 1923 was as an outside-right. A more recent England winger produced at Ayresome was *Eddie Holliday* in the early 1960s. Holliday, a nephew of Colin Grainger, later played with Sheffield Wednesday. In the early 1980s 'Boro produced another Irish favourite, *Terry Cochrane*, who took his tally of caps to 26 after his move from Burnley.

Barnsley have always had a reputation for producing notable wingers, but some of the biggest favourites have missed out on international recognition. The exception was *Johnny Kelly* (1946-52), who made over 200 appearances for the Reds and collected two Scottish caps. When he was signed from Morton, Kelly cost £4,000, but he soon proved himself worth it. That he was one of the finest outside-lefts in the business, scores of backs will vouch. It was said that the reason Alf Ramsey chose to play without wingers when he became England's manager was because he never recovered from the painful experience of trying to contain Kelly during one visit to Oakwell!

JOHN KELLY
Barnsley & Scotland

Like other clubs in the region, Barnsley often had to part with some of their best players, and they sold two of their finest wing prospects before the lads became internationals. Mexborough product *Eric Brook* managed some 80 outings before he and Fred Tilson left Oakwell for Manchester City in 1928. He went on to play 18 times for England in a great career which saw him figure in two FA Cup finals and win a League Championship medal. *Dick Spence* a local lad who made an immediate impact in the early 1930s, made 65 appearances and scored 30 goals before Barnsley sold him to Chelsea in 1934. However, before he went he helped the Reds win the Third Division (North) Championship – his last goal for the club (at New Brighton) being the one that clinched the title. At Chelsea he gained two England caps, but the only club honour that came his way during his long career was the one he won at Oakwell . . . and it always ensured that Spence remembered his native Yorkshire with affection!

*

Great Clubmen and Others

Barnsley have long had a reputation for finding outstanding wingers. It's a tradition which dates back to that golden era before the Great War. Solid defence was the basis of their success, but they had several fine forwards and some excellent wingers. The first of the great wing discoveries was *George Wall*, the sharp-shooting Geordie who arrived in 1904, made barely 60 appearances, and in 1906 was sold to Manchester United for a big fee. He went on to collect seven England caps and helped United win two League titles and the FA Cup. By the time Barnsley followed United to the Cup Final in 1910 they had two more fine wingers in *Wilf Bartrop* and *Tom Forman*; and when they collected another large fee with the sale of Forman to Spurs, they had a ready made replacement in *Bert Leavey*. Alas, Leavey suffered a broken leg at the quarter-final stage of that epic Cup run of 1912; but Barnsley promptly produced another "find", and within weeks

Jimmy Moore was a hero of the greatest triumph in club history when the Reds won the Cup in a replay at Bramall Lane.

Bartrop started the Oakwell tradition for wingers providing speed, skill and service, and he and his successors have given generations of Barnsley regulars countless hours of pleasure. First came local lad, *George Donkin* (1913-25), who clocked up some 250 appearances; and after him that bundle of Geordie brilliance, *Jimmy Curran* (1921-32), a speed merchant with a sharp eye for the half-chance who grabbed 75 goals in 260 games. *Tubby Ashton* (1927-36), with 300 appearances, was another great servant; and then, just before the war, *George Bullock* arrived from Stafford and played in some 120 matches before meeting a tragic death in a car crash during wartime service with the Fleet Air Arm.

In the late 1940s and early 1950s Barnsley boasted two of the game's finest wingers in Scots *Gavin Smith* and *Johnny Kelly*. Smith, who came from Dumbarton in 1939, gave the club magnificent service over some 15 years. During the war he played 230 times and scored 114 goals, and then went on to add another 260 games and some 40 goals to his record before quitting in 1953.

Of Smith's successors, perhaps the most popular was local lad *Arthur Kaye* (1951-59), who played for England Under-23s but never got the "full" cap many felt he deserved. Certainly he was the finest outside-right in the Second Division, and in over 270 appearances he not only scored more than 50 goals but turned in countless sparkling performances that had the fans cheering themselves hoarse. Later, after a spell at Blackpool, he returned to Yorkshire to play in some 170 games for Middlesbrough.

Johnny McCann (1955-8) and *Eddie O'Hara* (1962-4) maintained the club's Scottish tradition at outside-left. Later *George Hamstead* on the left and *Bob Earnshaw* on the right re-established the local link. Earnshaw, a Rotherham schoolteacher, clocked up some 250 appearances between 1962 and 1972, and though

he was never as popular as some of his more illustrious predecessors, he provided plenty of
excitement with his dribbling exploits. In the
early 1970s *Frank Sharp* restored the Scottish
tradition on the left, while Manchester man
Les Lea, who succeeded Earnshaw, played in
some 200 games.

Rotherham, too, have had some splendid
wingers in the past 40 years. One of the best
was *Jack Grainger* (1947-56), the outside-right
who played in well over 350 matches and
bagged a century of goals. Grainger was one of
a string of notable Millmoor forwards constantly sought by the big clubs, but he remained loyal to United in that era when they
boasted one of the best home-produced teams
in the country. A wing colleague who did leave
was *Len White*, who joined Newcastle for a big
fee in 1953. White was successfully converted
to centre-forward and hit more than 150 goals
for Newcastle; and later gave good service to
Huddersfield. Meanwhile, Grainger's successors have included *Barry Webster* (1955-61)
with some 200 games, *Richard Finney* (1973-
80) with around 250 appearances, and *Barry
Lyons*, who , after some 150 outings in the
mid-1960s, joined Nottingham Forest and later
had a good run at York.

Ian Butler (Rotherham and Hull).

It is intriguing to note that one forgotten
Rotherham outside-left had the distinction of
scoring a hat-trick on his debut in 1948; but
Tommy Lowder made only eight League appearances before moving on. Much better remembered are *Jimmy Rudd*, who was at York
before joining Rotherham in 1949, and local
product *Keith Bambridge* (1955-64), who spent
the first ten years of his career at Millmoor and
played in over 160 games.

Perhaps the best-known outside-left produced by Rotherham was *Ian Butler*, but after
about 100 appearances he moved to Hull in
1964 in the double deal which also took Ken
Houghton to Humberside. Butler played in
300 games for Hull before concluding his career at York and Barnsley. At Hull he followed in a line of notable wingers which included the likes of *Eddie Burbanks, Ken Harrison* and *Doug Clarke*. Of these, Burbanks, a
product of Denaby, was an outside-left, and
though he was at the veteran stage by the time
he arrived from Sunderland in 1948 he proved
an astute capture. Harrison was a member of
the same City side which enjoyed success in the
Carter era, and he made 250 appearances and
scored 50 goals before he left in 1954. A year
after Harrison's departure Doug Clarke arrived from Bury to begin a run in the No. 7
shirt which saw him make nearly 400 appearances and score over 80 goals before he left to
join Torquay in 1965.

A more recent Hull wing "find" was *Brian
Marwood*, who arrived as an apprentice in
1978. In 1984, after some 150 games, he joined
Wednesday for a six-figure fee; and by 1988 he
had moved on to Arsenal in a £600,000 deal.

Wednesday have had many fine wingers,
among them such splendid servants as *Alan
Finney* and *Derek Wilkinson*. Finney (1950-
66), who clocked up over 500 appearances and
claimed 90 goals, will always be associated with
his first inside partner, Albert Quixall, for they
arrived in the team together at 17. But Finney
had many partners, and his strength was his
ability to play on either flank with equal success. Wilkinson, too, was as much at home on

the right as the left wing, and, indeed, his adaptability was such that many of his 230 appearances were at centre-forward, and he scored more than 50 goals. Wilkinson was not the first Owls winger to succeed at centre-forward: *Dennis Woodhead* (1946-55) often made the switch in a career which saw him score 76 goals in 220 games. Incidentally, one of Woodhead's rivals for the No. 11 shirt in the late 1940s was *Charlie Tomlinson*; and though Tomlinson was limited to 77 games one of his 12 goals was among the most dramatic in club history. It was scored at Preston in 1949 and came exactly twelve seconds after the kick-off!

Two other Wednesday wingers of note were *Walter Rickett* and *Terry Curran*, who had in common the fact that they played with both Sheffield clubs. Rickett began his career with United, and, indeed, made his debut for the Blades against Wednesday in 1940 and scored with his very first kick! Later he played with Blackpool, appearing in the 1948 FA Cup final; but in 1949 he joined Wednesday and helped them win promotion twice, in 1950 and 1952, before concluding his career at Rotherham and Halifax. Curran also helped Wednesday win promotion (from the Third Division in 1980) and he enjoyed the best phase of his entire career at Hillsborough between 1979 and 1982. An often brilliant player, Curran could also be frustrating, and he seldom stayed long with one club. Having started his career at Doncaster and played with five clubs before joining Wednesday, he elected to leave and join United, but he soon moved on to Everton, and his later clubs included Huddersfield and Hull.

Another Wednesday winger often on the move was *Albert Broadbent*, who also played with Rotherham, Doncaster and Bradford PA among others but recorded over 100 goals in a career which spanned the years from 1952 to 1968. (*Neil Warnock*, now manager of Football League "babes" Scarborough, also travelled constantly as a player, and his other clubs in his native Yorkshire included Rotherham, Barnsley and York).

Curran is unlikely to be placed high on the list of Sheffield United wingers if only because his stay was so short. He never gave the service or made the impact of, for instance, *Harold Barton*, who played in some 200 games, hit 50 goals, and helped United reach the 1936 Cup final and win promotion in 1939. After Barton came Rickett on the right and George Jones or Colin Collindridge on the left; and later, in Ringstead and *Derek Hawksworth*, United had two of the best club wingers in Yorkshire in the 1950s. Hawksworth, who began and ended his career at Bradford City, made some 280 appearances for the Blades and scored nearly 100 goals. Later he had two years at Huddersfield, eventually returning to Valley Parade and bringing his career appearance tally to nearly 500 games.

Hawksworth was another man equally at home on either wing, and he also played at centre-forward. When United sold him to Huddersfield his replacement was *Ron Simpson*, who had played more than 100 times for Town. Simpson went on to make some 230 appearances for United between 1958 and 1964. About the time Simpson's Lane career was coming to an end and he was passing his No. 11 shirt to *Barry Hartle*, United found a long-term replacement for Len Allchurch on the other flank in former Barnsley Boys star, *Alan Woodward*. "Woody" was destined to earn a special niche in the club's records and proved to be one of the most loyal and consistent wingers United ever had. Between 1963 and 1978 he made over 570 appearances and scored 175 goals. Like Tunstall he had a terrific shot, and at his peak he was one of the most exciting forwards in the game, his link-up with Tony Currie at free-kicks and corners providing some of the most delightful moments of the 1970s. United have always been well served by wingers, from Walter Bennett in the 1890s to 250 game Colin Morris in the 1980s, but Woodward in his prime ranks with the best.

Huddersfield supporters would probably make the same claim for *Kevin McHale* (1956-68), who served the club quite brilliantly in

Alan Woodward – a record goal-scorer.

increasing trend towards greater freedom of movement for soccer stars. Thus the loyalty of such men as Woodward and McHale is less common than it was. If this pair are classic examples of essentially one-club wingers, it is appropriate to mention some others. Like *John Hall* (1962-73) with over 400 games (70 goals) for Bradford City; former Hull man *Charlie Atkinson* (1956-64) who made over 350 appearances (50 goals) for Bradford PA and finished at Valley Parade; and *Bill Depledge* (1946-55), nearly 300 games and over 60 goals for Bradford City. While wee *George Meek* later gave excellent service to Walsall, he made over 200 appearances for Leeds between 1952 and 1960. Bradford-born *Geoff Walker* spent eight years at Middlesbrough (1946-54), as did West Indian born *Lindy Delephena* (1949-57), who clocked up nearly 300 games and 100 goals. *Ron Walker* (1950-60) spent all his League career at Doncaster, making some 250 appearances and scoring 50 goals.

Leeds supporters who know their club's history will be familiar with the fact that the club has had two wingers called Cochrane: Irish international David, and before him a brilliant outside-left, *Tommy Cochrane* (1928-37), a Geordie who made some 260 appearances and formed a fine partnership with Billy Furniss. Yet good as Tommy was he took a long time to win round the Elland Road fans, who were unhappy when he displaced their great favourite, *Tom Mitchell* (1926-31). But Mitchell eventually moved on and found further crowd adulation awaiting him at York. Indeed, he settled in so well at Bootham that when his playing days were over he stayed on to become manager and then a director . . . perhaps the first ex-winger to join the board of a football club in Yorkshire!

more than 350 games and scored some 60 goals. This Darfield product was something of a boy wonder, for he stepped into the senior side at 16, and with him and Denis Law in the same team Town fans had plenty to cheer. Law moved on, but McHale remained to become a hero whose credentials assured him of a place in the club's hall of fame.

In lean times even the most famous clubs have to part with their best players, and the recent examples of McCall and John Hendrie leaving Bradford City for huge fees indicate an

8.   The Goal Kings

"It's goals that count!" is one of soccer's oldest cliches. Yet it remains true that football is all about scoring goals, and the most consistently successful and best-supported teams are those who please their followers by putting the ball in the net with greater frequency than their rivals. Thus the men with "the goal knack" have always been the most popular and publicised of players. They are the golden boys, the idols of the crowd; and those whose golas have been numbered in hundreds rather than dozens have passed into folklore, their feats and their fame living on long after they have departed the scene.

Some of the most prolific marksmen in Football League history have been associated with Yorkshire clubs: from such 300-goal stars of the inter-war years as *George Camsell* (Middlesbrough) and *Harry Johnson* (Sheffield United) to post-war "big shots" like *Brian Clough* (Middlesbrough), *Ken Wagstaff* (Hull) and *Peter Lorimer* (Leeds), who all topped the 200 mark.

Middlesbrough, who climbed from the Third to the First Division in two memorable years in the late 1980s after nearly going out of business in 1986, have had their share of trauma and triumph in a history which dates back to 1876; but they have consistently thrown up brilliant sharpshooters. The present-day supporter quite properly hails the success of Scot *Bernie Slaven*, whose 45 goals in the promotion campaigns of 1986-87 and 1987-88 brought joy to Teesside.

However, looking back, there are many famous names of yesteryear to remember. These include ex-pit boy *George Camsell* who was converted from a reserve winger into the most prolific sharpshooter of his era. Yet just before his promotion Camsell was on offer and would have gone to Barnsley for £300 had the Oakwell club not pulled out of the deal when they found they couldn't raise the cash! Then with 'Boro at the foot of Division Two in the early autumn of 1926, Camsell unexpectedly deputised for injured centre-forward Jimmy McClelland. By the end of the season 'Boro had clinched the Second Division championship and Camsell had made League history by scoring 59 goals (including a record nine hat-tricks) in only 37 games. In his career Camsell notched over 400 goals, including 371 in 488 games for 'Boro and 18 for England in only nine internationals. Dixie Dean later hit 60 goals in a season at Everton, but Camsell's 59 remains a Second Division record.

Middlesbrough have maintained the reputation established by Elliott and Camsell. *Micky Fenton* (1933-49) claimed well over 200

George Camsell
(Middlesbrough)

goals, including 70 in wartime matches. Later came *Brian Clough* (1952-61), who scored 197 goals in 213 League games before a £42,000 transfer took him to Sunderland. At Roker he raised his League tally to 252 before injury ended his playing days, but 'Boro supporters recall that 160 of his goals came in a brilliant four-season burst between 1956 and 1960, a period in which he also hit half-a-dozen FA Cup goals and scored five in one game for the Football League against the Irish League. Another local product, *Alan Peacock* (1954-63), enjoyed his best spell after succeeding Clough at centre-forward and bringing his tally to 126 in 218 League appearances before joining Leeds.

John Hickton was one 'Boro goal-king who never gained international honours, but he more than repaid the £20,000 he cost when signed from Sheffield Wednesday in 1966. A big-hearted lad who could play in defence or attack, Hickton really blossomed after moving to Ayresome, claiming 185 goals, including 159 in 400 League games, and helping push 'Boro from the Third to the First Division.

Ernest Hine (Barnsley)

Sheffield United's *Harry Johnson* did not depend on professional football for his livelihood; yet the steelworks metallurgist claimed 309 League goals in his career – 205 of them in 315 First Division games for the Blades before concluding his playing days with a century haul at Mansfield. Despite his lack of height and weight this son of an old United international was one of the most effective and popular forwards of his day, revelling in muddy conditions and playing with energy and enthusiasm which knew no bounds. He took the knocks in his stride and always bounced back; and he scored five goals in a match once, hit four seven times, and claimed 20 hat-tricks, plus one for the Football League XI.

Johnson's consistency kept *Jimmy Dunne* (1926-33) in the shadows for some years, but then the Irishman grabbed his chance and went on to score 143 goals in 173 League games. Dunne, who claimed 12 hat-tricks, scored many of his goals with his head from Tunstall crosses, so that "Tunnie-Dunnit!" became a popular catchphrase at Bramall Lane. In 1930-31 he established a Sheffield scoring record which still stands: his 51 goals comprising 41 in the League, five in the FA Cup, four headed in one County Cup match (against Wednesday!), and two for Ireland.

Until the emergence of winger Alan Woodward (mentioned in the previous chapter), who scored 158 League goals plus 17 in the League Cup and FA Cup, United's post-war aggregate scoring record has held by *"Doc" Pace* (1957-64) with 140 goals in 258 League games. The club had few more dependable and dedicated players than the man brought from Aston Villa in December 1957. His 163 League and Cup goals included six trebles, one four and a string of doubles, and he was the club's leading scorer in seven successive seasons.

In that 1976-77 campaign in which Woodward finally overtook Pace's total, a new goal-king emerged when *Keith Edwards* notched 18 goals to lead United's scoring charts for the first time. Edwards went on to claim 143 goals in 261 League appearances in two spells between 1975 and 1986. Edwards had the distinction of hitting 35 goals in 1981-82 when United won the Fourth Division championship, and this was the best by a United man since Dunne's 41 in 1930-31, being one more than Jock Dodds claimed in the Second Division in 1935-36. Edwards, who has also scored over 50 goals for Hull and played with Leeds, has taken his League tally to more than 200.

Barnsley's aggregate scoring record is still held by local discovery *Ernie Hine*, who hit 123 League goals (plus seven FA Cup) in two spells with the club between 1921 and 1938. Hine's speed, stamina and shooting power brought him 287 League goals (612 games) and his other clubs were Leicester, Huddersfield and Manchester United. He also scored five in six games for England, and it was after his return to Oakwell in 1934 that he took Barnsley's record from the legendary George Lilleycrop (92 League goals plus 12 FA Cup, 1907-13). In modern times only *Lol Chappell* (1952-59), with 96 in 230 matches, has rivalled Hine.

In the years between the wars Huddersfield had a succession of goal-heroes, including *J. G. Cock* (sold to Chelsea in 1919 to pay the wage-bill), *Dave Mangnall* (who had a run of 33 goals in 34 games in 1922-23), and *Charles Wilson* (1922-26); but the greatest of them all was surely *George Brown* (1921-29), who collected a hat-trick of League Championship medals and eight England caps while at Leeds Road. In the third Championship season, 1925-26, Brown's 35 League goals equalled the record set by Sheffielder Sam Taylor in the Second Division promotion campaign of 1919-20; and Brown went on to claim the aggregate record with 142 goals in 214 games. He also played for Aston Villa, Burnley, Leeds and Darlington, and his brilliance in the air and fine positional skills enabled him to snatch 268 League goals in his career.

In post-war years *Jimmy Glazzard* (1946-56), with 139 goals in 299 League matches, has come closest to taking Brown's record. Indeed, some reference books insist that he equalled Brown's tally. Glazzard claimed an

Frank Keetley, a Yorkshire goal king. His brother Tom scored 180 goals for Doncaster Rovers.

additional 33 goals in wartime games, plus 12 in the FA Cup, so his overall tally of 184 puts him in a special class so far as Town supporters are concerned; and certainly he was one of the great favourites in that fine Town side of the early 1950s. His 30 goals in the Second Division promotion campaign of 1952-53 (he hit 92 in League and Cup in a three-season run) is a total challenged since only by Ian Robins (25 in 1979-80) and Alan Gowling (24 in 1973-74); while Les Massie's 98 goals in 334 games between 1953 and 1966 is the nearest anyone has come to equalling his League aggregate.

Doncaster Rovers' aggregate League scoring record is still held after 60 years by *Tom Keetley* (1923-29) with 180. Keetley was a member of a unique family of footballing brothers (they all had spells at Belle Vue) who hold the remarkable distinction of having scored 500 League goals between them. Tom, who started out with Bradford PA, hit 278 with four clubs; Charles scored 115 with three clubs, 108 of them for Leeds United between 1927

Left: Ken Wagstaff, one of the biggest favourites of Hull City in post-war years.
Right: Andrew Wilson, who has held Sheffield Wednesday's aggregate scoring record for some seventy years.

and 1934; Frank's 75 included 31 for Doncaster; Harold scored all of his 23 for Rovers; and Joe hit 18 with five clubs. Tom's goals for Rovers included eleven hat-tricks and four fours, plus a remarkable six-goal performance in a Third Division (North) game at Ashington in February 1929. Brother Frank also hit a six – in 21 minutes! – for Lincoln in 1933 when Halifax Town were on the receiving end.

Bert Tindill (1946-57) and *Alick Jeffrey* (1954-56 and 1963-69) are the only Rovers men to come near to rivalling Keetley's record in modern times. Tindill was a wartime discovery who had some 50 outings (15 goals) before beginning a remarkably consistent League career which saw him make 400 appearances and score 122 goals (133 in League and Cup); and

he held the post-war scoring record until Jeffrey made his famous comeback in the 1960s. Jeffrey was the boy wonder who made his League debut at 15 and had chalked up some 70 appearances (38 goals) when a double fracture of a leg in an England Under-23 game seemed to have finished his career. However, with the help of George Raynor, after seven "lost" years during which he played in places as far apart as Skegness and Sydney, Jeffrey eventually fought his way back and went on to lift his League tally to 129 goals in 262 games (140 in League and Cup).

Hull City have boasted two 200-goal men in modern times: and between them *Ken Wagstaff* and *Chris Chilton* claimed some 430 goals for City in League and Cup. Wagstaff managed 269 League goals in 550 matches, having scored 96 for Mansfield before his £40,000 move to Hull in November 1964 shortly before City splashed another £40,000 to sign Butler and Houghton from Rotherham. For City Wagstaff hit 173 League goals plus 39 in Cupties; while Chilton, who cost only a £10 signing on fee, clocked up 195 goals in 415 League appearances between 1960 and 1971, plus 20 in Cup games. Chilton broke up their dynamic partnership in August 1971 when he joined Coventry for £92,000; but an early injury prevented him taking his tally of League goals past 200.

Burly Scottish international *Andrew Wilson* (1900-20) has held Sheffield Wednesday's aggregate scoring record for some 70 years, and his tally of 199 League goals in 500 games seems likely to remain unchallenged for a long time yet. Wilson's full haul was 216 in 545 League and Cup appearances, and he helped Wednesday win two League Championships and the FA Cup. Leading challengers among his colleagues were *Fred Spiksley* (116 goals) and *Harry Chapman* (102). A later Owls title-winning side included the free-scoring wingers Rimmer (140) and Hooper (136); while in modern times best of the hot-shots have been *Redfern Froggatt* (1946-60) with 149 League and Cup goals and *John Fantham* (1958-69) with 167. Froggatt, son of an old Wednesday captain, was a fine inside-forward who was as much a maker as a taker of goals; Fantham was always the opportunist, the man with a natural instinct for being in the right place at the right time. Fantham, who notched his 141st League goal in 1968 to take the post-war record from Froggatt just a year before he left to join Rotherham, was unlucky not to gain more than one England cap. Froggatt played five times for England.

As mentioned in the previous chapter, Leeds United's record marksman is *Peter Lorimer* with 237 goals in some 700 League and Cup games. Lorimer was able to claim the League aggregate record by scoring 17 times after his surprise return to Elland Road in 1983

to bring his tally to 168. However, it will be noted that he required some 500 games to clinch the record, while the previous holder, *John Charles*, hit his 153 in just over 300 League games.

Few would deny that Charles, "the gentle giant", was the greatest player Leeds ever had: the complete footballer, capped 38 times by Wales and as much at home at the heart of defence as leading the attack. His switch to centre forward was an inspired move, and in one spell between 1952 and 1957 he scored 150 goals in a run which saw him miss only ten of 217 games before his transfer to Juventus for what was then a world record £65,000 fee. In 1962 he returned briefly to Leeds, but soon went back to Italy.

Charles claimed United's record haul for a season with 42 in 1953-54, and his 38 in 1956-57 is still the club's best in Division One. The previous best was 35 by *Tom Jennings* in 1926-27, but, remarkably, Jennings' performance (which included three successive hat-tricks) was not sufficient to save Leeds from relegation! Jennings (1925-31), one of the most courageous players United ever had, hit 117 goals in 174 games.

Rotherham's fine homespun team of the early post-war years has already been mentioned, but it is appropriate here to note that four of their forwards – *Gladstone Guest, Jack Shaw, Wally Ardron* and *Jack Grainger* – totted up almost 500 League and Cup goals between them; and that figure excludes the 129 goals Ardron scored for the Millers in the war years! Guest, a fine inside-forward and captain, actually holds the club's aggregate League scoring record with 130 goals; but it is interesting to note that while he managed only three in the FA Cup, colleague Jack Shaw notched 124 League goals plus 18 in the FA Cup to lift his overall total to 142, plus 15 in wartime. Shaw later scored 27 for Sheffield Wednesday. Ardron claimed 96 League goals in only 122 matches, and his seven in the FA Cup coupled with his wartime tally meant he scored over 230 in seven years before his move

Kevin Hector, the last of the great sharpshooters at Bradford Park Avenue before the club left the Football League.

to Nottingham Forest in 1949. With Forest he lifted his League aggregate to 219. Grainger's haul of 118 goals included ten in the FA Cup.

Ardron's 38 in 1946-47 remains Rotherham's best in a League season, though his tally of 40 in League and Cup that term was bettered by Shaw, whose 46 in that memorable 1950-51 Division Three (North) championship campaign included nine in the Cup. Before the war Billy Hick hit 30 in 1930-31 and Bramham 31 in 1938-39; but the only man to top 30 since Shaw was Ronnie Burke with 32 in 1953-54.

Guest and Grainger at Millmoor epitomised a brand of loyalty among players which was once fairly commonplace in the game.

York, too, have had many similarly long-serving men, some of whom have been fine goal-getters. *Norman Wilkinson* began his career as an amateur with Hull, but after National Service he joined York in 1954 and went on to clock up 354 League appearances and claim the club's aggregate record with 125 goals. He took the record from another great stalwart, *Billy Fenton* (118 goals in 258 games, 1951-57), who in turn had snatched the honour from *Alf Patrick* (111 goals in 234 games, 1946-52).

In some ways the records of Patrick and Fenton are more impressive, but Wilkinson marked his first term at Bootham by scoring 23 goals, including four in that famous run to the FA Cup semi-finals in 1955. Yet the man who took the bulk of the bouquets that year was ex-Sheffield United man, *Arthur Bottom*, whose 38 goals included eight in the Cup. Bottom claimed 91 League goals in only 137 games between 1954 and 1958, and his 31 in 1955-56 enabled him to share the club's League record for a season with Billy Fenton, who had had the same total in 1951-52.

Before Fenton the club's best in a season was 29 by *Reg Baines* in 1932-33. Baines later had spells with Sheffield United and Doncaster Rovers before returning to York. In later years *Paul Aimson* also had two spells at Bootham, registering 98 goals in 210 League games; but the nearest Aimson got to the club record was 26 in 1970-71; and *Jimmy Weir* (28) in 1961-62 and *John Byrne* (27) in 1983-84 both went closer.

Bobby Campbell recently claimed the Bradford City aggregate League scoring record which *Frank O'Rourke* (88) had held since 1913. The much-travelled Campbell registered 76 goals in 148 games in his first spell at Valley Parade (1981-84), and following his quick return from Derby claimed the record during a run of 126 matches which saw him lift his tally to 121 before he left again to join Wigan. Campbell's other clubs have included Huddersfield, Sheffield United and Halifax.

Campbell managed only three goals in 33 games for Halifax in two spells in the 1970s, and so never even began to challenge the aggregate record of *Ernest Dixon* (129 goals, 1922-30) or the season's best at The Shay held by *Albert Valentine*, whose 34 in 1934-35 took Town desperately close to the Third Division (North) championship. *Bill Atkins*, with 71 in two spells between 1965 and 1972, has been the most successful of the modern marksmen, taking the post-war record from *Des Frost* (1951-53), who managed 55 goals in 117 games. *Les Massie*, with 25 goals in 1967-68, has been the nearest to equalling Valentine's record.

Tom Keetley, with 40 goals in 1928-29, claimed Doncaster's best in a season in 1927-28, but the record passed to *Clarrie Jordan* in that famous Third Division (North) championship season of 1946-47 – the year the ex-miner bagged 42 goals, including four hat-tricks. Soon afterwards Jordan moved to Sheffield Wednesday, but knee trouble halted his run of success. His Rovers record survives. *Alick Jeffrey's* 36 in 1964-65 has been the best of recent years. Incidentally, *Peter Kitchen* (1970-77) twice topped the scoring charts, and his total of 89 in 228 League games puts him in line behind Jeffrey and Tindill in the post-war table.

Sheffield Wednesday have had many prolific marksmen other than those previously discussed, including *Jimmy Trotter* (1921-29), whose 114 goals in 160 games included 37 in each of two separate seasons and two five-goal performances; *Jack Ball*, whose 94 in 135 games included a record eleven penalty conversions in 1931-32; and *Jack Allen* (1927-31), whose 85 goals in 115 games helped Wednesday win the League Championship twice. *Roy Shiner* (96) and *Jack Sewell* (92) were "big shot" favourites in the 1950s, but the biggest scoring sensation of that decade was *Derek Dooley*, the 6ft 2ins giant who claimed 63 goals in 63 games before his career came to a tragic end in 1953 when a broken leg became infected and it had to be amputated. In 1951-52 Dooley hit 47 goals in 31 appearances and shot the Owls to the Second Division championship. He took the club's scoring record from Trotter and joined Trotter and Jimmy Dailey on the club's five-goals-in-a-match list. His only failure was in not equalling *Douglas Hunt's* 1938 feat of scoring six times in a game!

We cannot refer to Wednesday goal-aces without mentioning *Jackie Robinson*, for though he managed only 39 in 119 League games he made a strong claim to lasting fame by scoring some 90 goals in only 100 matches in the war years. Indeed, in 1942-43, when Wednesday reached the final of the League North Cup, Robinson scored 35 goals, including six hat-tricks, thanks to the support of team-mates Cockcroft and Frank Melling. Capped by England at 19, Robinson was one of the most brilliant and complete forwards ever to play for Wednesday.

Eddie Quigley (1947-49) played only 78 games for the Owls but hit over 50 goals. More recently *Gary Bannister* (1981-84) claimed 66 in 142 matches, while lanky *Lee Chapman* hit more than 80 in 180 outings before leaving to play in France in 1988.

We should not overlook *David McLean*, who in 1911 became Wednesday's first £1,000 player and went on to score 100 goals in only 147 games before moving to Bradford in 1920. At Park Avenue it was David's brother, *George McLean*, who was the great idol of the inter-war years with some 140 goals between 1922 and 1930. McLean later played for Huddersfield, and it was soon after his move to Leeds Road that he claimed four goals when Town registered their record League victory with a 10-1 crushing of Blackpool in December 1930.

McLean's best in a season at Bradford was 27 in 1928-29, but this could not match *Ken McDonald's* 43 in 1925-26, a record which survived until 1965-66 when *Kevin Hector* hit 44. Hector was the last of the great sharpshooters at Park Avenue before the club left the Football League, and his 113 goals in 176 League games prompted Derby to pay £40,000 for his services – a fee which proved to be money well spent.

There were two Bradford records which neither McLean nor Hector could match: one

Jim Fryatt's feat of April 1964 when he scored after only four seconds in the game with Tranmere; the other *George Henson's* six-goal performance against Blackburn Rovers in January 1938.

David Layne still holds Bradford City's record for goals in a season (34 in 1961-62), but Layne is best remembered for having scored 58 goals in 81 games for Sheffield Wednesday before his career was dramatically halted following exposure of his notorious betting coup scandal by a Sunday newspaper in 1964. Layne's life-ban was lifted in 1972, but by then his best days were behind him.

Sheffield United's other notable marksmen have included the previously mentioned Gillespie (139), Tunstall (135), Hagan (111), and Pickering (111); plus "Lincolnshire poacher" *Joe Kitchen* (114 goals, 1908-21) and *Jock Dodds*, who was signed on a free transfer from Huddersfield and scored 124 goals between 1934 and 1939 when he was sold to Blackpool for £10,000.

Several United men have also been associated with Leeds, including *Harold Brook*, who scored 107 goals for the Blades between 1940 and 1954 and later claimed 47 after moving to Elland Road; and *Len Browning*, who began his career at Leeds (46 goals, 1946-52)

David Layne (Bradford City and Sheffield Wednesday).

and finished it at Bramall Lane when illness ended his playing days. More recently, *Mick Jones* cost £100,000 when he joined Leeds in 1967 after scoring 63 goals in 149 games for the Sheffield club. Jones, who gained two of his three England caps while at Bramall Lane, became a big favourite at Leeds, for whom he scored 111 goals in 309 games and made a big contribution to the success enjoyed by *Allan Clarke*. A £165,000 buy from Leicester in 1969, Clarke proved himself one of the great goal-poachers of his era, scoring 151 goals in 364 games before moving to Barnsley in 1978.

The Leeds-Barnsley link prompts reference to *Russell Wainscoat*, the Maltby lad who had the distinction of scoring a hat-trick on his League debut for Barnsley in 1920. After notching 59 goals in 153 games Wainscoat was sold to Middlesbrough in 1923 for a big fee; but it was at Leeds between 1924 and 1931 that he enjoyed his best spell, scoring 93 goals in 226 matches for United and collecting his only England cap.

Barnsley have had many fine marksmen on their books down the years, from the 1912 FA Cup final heroes, the 104-goal *George Lilleycrop* (they called him "Goalcrop") and 62-goal *Harry Tufnell* (who later became York's first manager) to 80-goal *Joe Halliwell* (1913-27) and 78-goal *Brough Fletcher* (1914-29) through to such moderns as *Johnny Evans, Mick Butler* and *Ronnie Glavin*. Nearly 40 years have passed since *Cec McCormack* claimed the season's best with 33 goals in 1950-51 – the term in which he joined *Frank Eaton, Peter Cunningham* and *Beaumont Asquith* in the line-up of Reds favourites who have scored five goals in a match. Before McCormack the season record was held by another North Easterner, *Abe Blight*, who notched 31 in that Third Division (North) championship triumph of 1933-34. Strange to think that McCormack was one man Middlesbrough let go, because they thought he was too small to make the grade. Little Cec proved a few people wrong, but then so did Blight until his career was brought to a premature end by injury.

The biggest Barnsley favourites in the post-war era were probably *George Robledo* and *Tommy Taylor*. Chilean-born Robledo cracked 48 goals in 96 wartime games before starting his Football League career with a hat-trick in that 1946-47 season when he finished with 22 goals. By 1949 Robledo and his brother Ted were on their way to Newcastle, and the scene was set for the emergence of local boy Taylor. However, Taylor made only 44 League appearances and scored 26 goals before he joined Manchester United for £1 short of £30,000. At Old Trafford, Taylor blossomed into greatness, with 112 League goals and 16 goals for England in 19 games; but then tragedy struck and he was one of eight Busby Babes to perish in the 1958 Munich Air disaster.

The earlier reference to Wainscoat reminds me that when this old-time Oakwell favourite concluded his career at Hull he showed that he had lost none of his guile and flair, and he formed a notable partnership with *Bill McNaughton*, the former Barking carpenter who arrived on Humberside from Gateshead. In 1932-33 the pair notched 60 goals between them to help City win the Third Division (North) Championship. McNaughton's 39 goals that term remains a club record, with *Bill Bradbury's* 30 in 1958-59 the best since. Indeed, it is worthy of note that, good as Chilton and Wagstaff were as a duo, they only twice topped 50 League goals between them - in 1964-65 and 1965-66. Wagstaff didn't have the consolation of having taken the record at his previous club, Mansfield, for that honour belonged to *Ted Harston* with 55 in 1936-37. Harston hailed from Monk Bretton, and he was cast off by both Sheffield Wednesday and Barnsley (at Oakwelll after scoring six goals in a reserve game); which just goes to show that sometimes even in Yorkshire we fail to recognise talent when we see it!

GEORGE
ROBLEDO
Barnsley

Yorkshire Soccer Milestones

Clubs' formation dates: **Sheffield Wednesday** (1867) **Middlesbrough** (1876); **Doncaster Rovers** (1879); **Scarborough** (1879); **Rotherham United** (as Thornhill United, 1884); **Barnsley** (1887); **Sheffield United** (1889); **Bradford City** (1903); **Leeds City** (1904); **Hull City** (1904); **Bradford PA** (1907); **Huddersfield Town** (1908); **Halifax Town** (1911); **Leeds United** (1919); **York City** (1922).
Note: Leeds City were banished from the game by the FA in 1919 and Leeds United came into being almost immediately. Rotherham United were created in 1925 with the amalgamation of Rotherham Town and Rotherham County.

HONOURS LIST
FA Cup Winners:
Sheffield Wednesday 1896
Sheffield United 1899
Sheffield United 1902
Sheffield Wednesday 1907
Bradford City 1911
Barnsley 1912
Sheffield United 1915
Huddersfield Town 1922
Sheffield United 1925
Sheffield Wednesday 1935
Leeds United 1972

FA Cup runners up: Sheff Wednesday 1890; Sheff United 1901; Barnsley 1910; Huddersfield 1920; Huddersfield 1928; Huddersfield 1930; Sheff United 1936; Huddersfield 1938; Leeds United 1965; Sheff Wednesday 1966; Leeds United 1970; Leeds United 1973.

Division One Champions:
Sheffield United 1897-98
Sheffield Wednesday 1902-03
Sheffield Wednesday 1903-04
Huddersfield Town 1923-24
Huddersfield Town 1924-25
Huddersfield Town 1925-26
Sheffield Wednesday 1928-29
Sheffield Wednesday 1929-30
Leeds United 1968-69
Leeds United 1973-74

Division One runners-up: Sheff United 1896-97; Sheff United 1899-1900; Huddersfield 1926-27; Huddersfield 1927-28; Huddersfield 1933-34; Sheff Wednesday 1960-61; Leeds United 1964-65; Leeds United 1965-66; Leeds United 1969-70; Leeds United 1970-71; Leeds United 1971-72.

Division Two Champions:
Sheff Wednesday 1899-1900
Bradford City 1907-08
Leeds United 1923-24
Sheff Wednesday 1925-26
Middlesbrough 1926-27
Middlesbrough 1928-29
Sheff Wednesday 1951-52
Sheff United 1952-53
Sheff Wednesday 1955-56
Sheff Wednesday 1958-59
Leeds United 1963-64
Huddersfield Town 1969-70
Middlesbrough 1973-74

Division Two runners-up: Sheff United 1892-93; Middlesbrough 1901-02; Bradford PA 1913-14; Huddersfield Town 1919-20; Leeds United 1927-28; Leeds United 1931-32; Sheff United 1938-39; Sheff Wednesday 1949-50; Huddersfield 1952-53; Leeds United 1955-56; Sheff United 1960-61; Sheff United 1970-71; Sheff Wednesday 1983-84. Promoted from Div 2 after play offs: Middlesbrough 1987-88.

Division Three (North) Champions:
Bradford PA 1927-28
Bradford City 1928-29
Hull City 1932-33
Barnsley 1933-34
Doncaster R 1934-35
Barnsley 1938-39
Doncaster R 1946-47
Hull City 1948-49
Doncaster R 1949-50
Rotherham United 1950-51
Barnsley 1954-55

Division Three (North) runners-up: Bradford PA 1922-23; Bradford PA 1925-26; Halifax Town 1934-35; Doncaster Rovers 1937-38 and 1938-39; Rotherham United 1946-47, 1947-48; Barnsley 1953-54.

Division Three Champions:
Hull City 1965-66
Rotherham United 1980-81
Bradford City 1984-85

Promoted from Division Three: Hull City (runners up) 1958-59; Middlesbrough (runners up)1966-67); York City 1973-74; Sheff Wednesday 1979-80; Barnsley (runners up) 1980-81; Huddersfield Town 1982-83; Sheff United 1983-84; Hull City 1984-85; Middlesbrough (runners up) 1986-87.

Division Four Champions:
Doncaster R 1965-66
Doncaster R 1968-69
Huddersfield 1979-80
Sheff United 1981-82
York City 1983-84

Promoted from Division Four: York City 1958-59; Bradford PA 1960-61; York City 1964-65; Barnsley (runners up) 1967-68; Halifax Town (runners up) 1968-69; Bradford City 1968-69; York City 1970-71; Rotherham United 1974-75; Bradford City 1976-77; Barnsley 1978-79; Doncaster Rovers 1980-81; Bradford City (runners-up) 1981-82; Hull City (runners up) 1982-83; Doncaster Rovers (runners up) 1983-84.

Football League Cup: Winners, Leeds United 1968. Runners-up, Rotherham, 1961.

European Cup: Leeds United runners-up 1974-75
Euro Cup-Winners' Cup: Leeds United runners-up 1972-73
Fairs Cup: Leeds United winners 1968 and 1971, runners-up 1967.
FA Amateur Cup: Middlesbrough winners 1895 and 1898; Sheffield FC winners 1904.

Pipped for promotion to Division One on goal-average:
Hull City 1909-10; Barnsley 1921-22; Sheffield United 1937-38; and Rotherham United 1954-55.

Bibliography

Soccer at War 1939-45, by Jack Rollin (Collins Willow).

Hotbed of Soccer, by Arthur Appleton (Hart-Davies).

Football Players' Records 1946-84 by Barry J. Hugman (Newnes).

The Encyclopaedia of Association Football, by Maurice Golesworthy (Hale).

A Century of English International Football 1872-1972 by Morley Farror &
Douglas Lamming (Hale).

Oakwell: the Official History of Barnsley FC, by Grenville Firth (Firth, 1978).

Leeds United: A Complete Record, 1919-86, by Martin Jarred & Malcolm Macdonald (Breedon Books).

Wednesday! by Keith Farnsworth
(Sheffield City Libraries).

*Sheffield Wednesday: A Complete Record,
1867-1987*, by Keith Farnsworth
(Breedon Books).

*The Avenue: Bradford PA Pictorial History
and Record*, by Malcolm Hartley and Tim
Chapman (Temple Nostalgia Press).

Rothman's Football Yearbooks, Sheffield
Telegraph, Playfair and News of the World
Football Annuals.

Acknowledgements

The author wishes to thank all those people
consulted during the preparation of this book,
including Peter Darling, Keith Littlewood,
Malcolm Hartley, Denis Clarebrough and the
late Dick Williamson. Special thanks to his
wife, Linda, for extensive help in reading the
manuscript and proofs.

Photographs and Illustrations:
Those illustrations not provided by the author
himself have been supplied by the following (to
whom thanks are offered for permission to rep-
roduce them): Sheffield Newspapers, Stuart
Machin, Keith Littlewood, and several ex-
players.

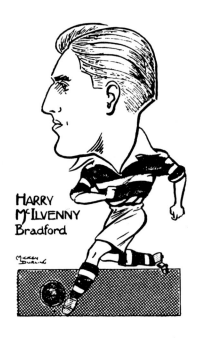

HARRY
McILVENNY
Bradford